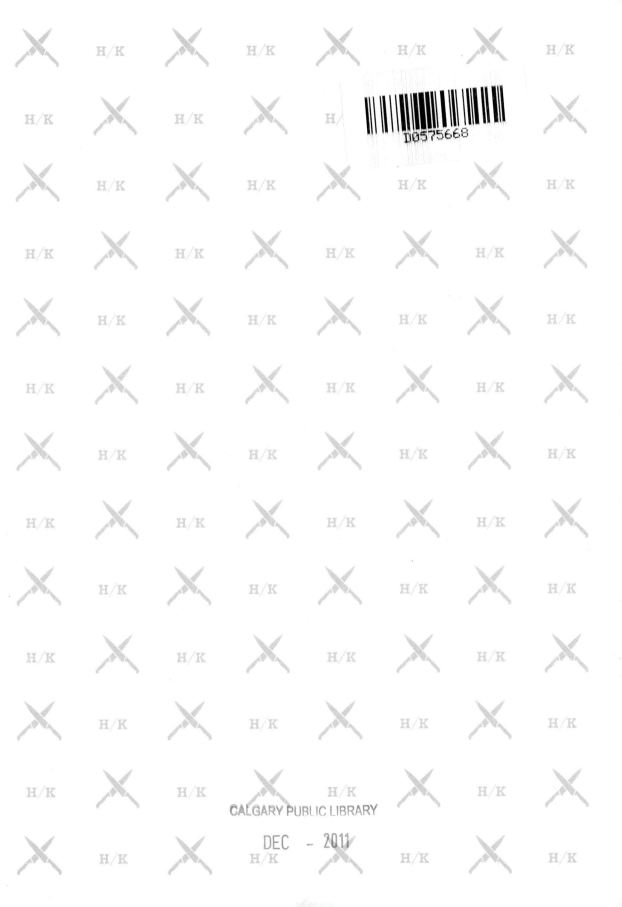

Salad Daze

THE HOT KNIVES
VEGETARIAN COOKBOOK

MARK BATTY PUBLISHER
NEW YORK CITY

The Hot Knives Vegetarian Cookbook: Salad Daze
by Alex Brown & Evan George

Design: Jen Wick Design Studio
Photography: Amanda Marsalis
Editor: Jake Davis
Production/Design Director: Christopher D Salyers

Typeset in HFJ Whitney and Vitesse

Library of Congress Control # 2011924564

ISBN: 978-1-9356133-3-6

10 9 8 7 6 5 4 3 2 1 First edition

Printed and bound in China through Asia Pacific Offset

Mark Batty Publisher
68 Jay Street, Suite 410
Brooklyn, NY 11201
www.markbattypublisher.com

Distributed outside North America by:
Thames & Hudson Ltd
181A High Holborn
London WC1V 7QX
United Kingdom
Tel: 00 44 20 7845 5000
Fax: 00 44 20 7845 5055
www.thameshudson.co.uk

You never know what is enough unless you know what is more than enough.

— *William Blake*

Introduction

Cooking for a blog is a funny thing: it's so much lazier than the cooking we've done in restaurants. Absent are the tiffs with servers, the maddening cricket of printing tickets, that greasy kitchen cologne we wear home, and the climactic spine-crimping buzz that only untangles once

> **We'll probably palm a Napa cabbage, fondle some kale, sniff chives, and snag apples, pears, and a fennel bulb that flies its freak-flag of bushy green fronds sticking out from the bag under our arm.**

the last plate hits the window. Our home kitchens by contrast are cozy, ordered temples. Stacks of bone-white towels; spice jars eternally half full; and the comforting bleed of a Dinosaur Jr. guitar solo rising above the crackle of shallots hitting greased cast-iron. Weekends are our Sabbath.

On Saturday mornings we slip out of our beds, grab the mess of canvas bags from the kitchen wall, and steer toward our Silver Lake farmers market while the streets are mercifully empty. Once there

it's first things first: strong coffee from the stand at the end of a long row of vendors. Our friend Mitch pulls a shot of biting Guatemalan espresso and hands it over in a brown porcelain saucer. Standing back to sip, we stare out at Downtown LA's skyline rising above the fruit and veggie rainbows that crisscross the market, feeling like kids let into the den to watch Saturday morning cartoons.

We'll probably palm a Napa cabbage, fondle some kale, sniff chives, and snag apples, pears, and a fennel bulb that flies its freak-flag of bushy green fronds from the bags under our arms. Some weeks, we find ripe, orange Italian frying peppers or massive purple grapes. Other times the Korean farmers ply us with water spinach and okra. Fresh eggs are involved, and flowers for our ladies. Every so often, we get a new weapon: Romanesco broccoli, purple asparagus, breakfast radishes, epazote.

Next comes a leisurely laptop sesh at our kitchen table, reading weirdo tenets of cooking from far-flung corners of the web—like the best way to peel fresh banana flower, why it's key to use malted barley syrup for bagels, or how much agar agar to mix per ounce of water. Then we lumber for our knives. Kitchen jamming, we find, is best done in monk-silence, powwowing at critical moments of decision making and boilovers. ("Should we try frying the capers?" "Oh fuck yes.") When inspiration strikes, the one who's not manning the cast-iron grabs a camera for posterity's sake. Food gets plated and trussed up for a

Alex (left) and Evan (right)
commence their Saturday ritual.

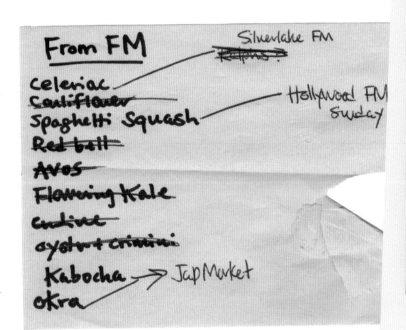

From FM

Celeriac
~~Cauliflower~~
Spaghetti Squash
~~Red bell~~
~~Avos~~
~~Flowering Kale~~
~~Endive~~
~~oyster + crimini~~

Kabocha → Jap Market
Okra

Silverlake FM
~~Ralphs~~

Hollywood FM
Sunday

hasty close-up, then disappears in quick succession. And that's it—that's what we've done most weekends for six years. We buy vegetables and we play with them, filtering it all through one giddy stoner kaleidoscope that has become our home-cooking philosophy: heady, hearty, vegetative.

Our approach has taken time to ripen; we did not pay for culinary school or spend a year in France, Italy, or Japan. Naw: the closest thing to a cooking primer we ever received were the two years of prep-cook shifts in the mess hall at our liberal arts college, where we learned how to deftly break down frozen chicken breasts, brew five gallons of Alfredo sauce, and diligently refill the salad bar. How well did this go over with two anti-war, feminist hooligans who didn't eat animals? Well enough that it cemented our pinko dietary tendencies. Yet we wanted nothing more than to slash and burn things at a stove. So we started cooking up regular drunk brunches for a gaggle of girlfriends in our dorm room. Back then our limited repertoire included two-step dishes like tortilla española, and honey-crusted tofu cubes. Or taco-truck burritos sprinkled with psilocybin mushrooms. But after getting our history and philosophy degrees it was time to pay rent. We entered the world of LA restaurant jobs: cafes and coffee shops, halfway decent bistros, a French place run by Koreans, a bakery commanded by a lady with insane fake tits. We have some okay scars: Alex lost part of a finger to butter-poached hash browns (duuuude!), and once Evan slammed a ticket spike clean through his right hand (luckily there

was salt, lemon, and whiskey to clean it, thanks Doug!). In more formative years, we also had the pleasure to work the line (and season the bar stools) at the very best meatless kitchen in Los Angeles, Elf Cafe. Taught by our friendships with a few vegetarian masterminds—and tried by fire—we are very much free-style mercenaries. Rather than butter-scald ourselves forever in the service of others, we started looking for ways to cook more in our own two kitchens.

Becoming Bloggers

So in 2005, we started a newspaper column about vegetarian cooking, and with it a blog. One lived; one died. The Hot Knives blog was mostly meant to

> Back then our limited repertoire included two-step dishes like tortilla española, and honey-crusted tofu cubes. Or taco-truck burritos sprinkled with psilocybin mushrooms.

chronicle our drunken brunch experiments. But once we got a couple decent cameras and befriended the internet intelligentsia of Portland, Oregon—Urbanhonking.com, who still hosts us today—we were full-on food blogging.

Clockwise: Evan and Alex shopping; food styling with Votar.

The idea behind Hot Knives has always been fall-down-drunk simple: goof off in the kitchen until we hit an ah-ha moment—like how to make the perfect vegan tea sandwich—while people at home watch. New schemes came quick: we'd review beers, pair those beers with cheese and songs, cater friends' parties, and write about it. Our first big cooking gig as bloggers was flipping animal-style seitan burgers at a rock 'n' roll "summer camp" in a warehouse parking lot in Downtown LA that promoters had covered with astro turf and water slides. Our second was competing in the Grilled Cheese Invitational against ladies in

Sure, nowadays everyone and their mom's favorite Food Network chef talks about vegetable-focused cooking. That's nice, but as long as their pancetta in those Trader Joe's Brussels sprouts, we're gonna call bullshit.

Kraft Singles mini-skirts who squirted breast milk on their weed ghee sammiches. Getting the picture?

Another year we decided, why not host a forty-mile bike ride around Los Angeles dedicated to beer? We would take several dozen strangers who found us through the web on a sweaty tour of our favorite liquor stores, and afterward we'd have them over to drink ninety-nine bottles and then we'd roast hot nuts for them on the patio.

Despite all the drunken videos, the noise music, and the obscure thistle-rennet cheeses, we've always taken great pains to plant ourselves in the camp of web users who share ideas, not dictate them. We hawk food tricks and kitchen tips, not food porn. We'd rather out-think you than out-cook you.

And what could be smarter than ways to make vegetables magic without using processed, store-bought crud and animal parts? The one Great Lie perpetrated on us all during this foodie craze is that there's still a place for dumb convenience in the modern kitchen. Pre-minced garlic, plastic-wrapped mirepoix, already cleaned shrimp, or (god forbid!) vegetable stock in expensive milk cartons: we call bullshit! You want a smaller carbon footprint, or a lap-band replacement, or a place to meet hot singles who can cook? All you need is a farmers market. Which is great, because you'll also find veggies, in all their rumpled green, knobby-bulby goodness there.

We let vegetables do all the talking: we believe in letting them shine through a simple kitchen prism of basic know-how, witty ideas, sharp knives, quality oil, spices, vinegars, and homemade sauces; then we pair 'em with strong booze. Sure, nowadays everyone and their mom's favorite Food Network chef talks about vegetable-focused cooking. That's nice, but as long as there's pancetta in those Trader Joe's Brussels sprouts, we're gonna call bullshit (we call bullshit a lot). This is about feeling stoned on the awesome power of properly cooked produce. That's the salad daze.

On Fall and Winter

So why would anyone want to eat salad-sy meals in winter? For one thing, vegetables are how we measure time and the passing of the year.

garlic
ginger
cilantro
lemongrass

Clockwise: Evan and Alex tour a Portland farmers market; Alex scooping gelato for beer floats; herb shopping.

Clockwise: Evan and Alex fingering
potatoes; Alex buying Napa cabbage;
Evan cooking with beer.

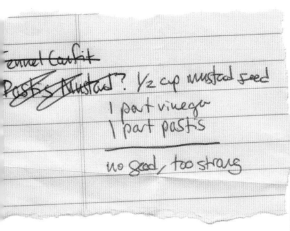

Fennel Confit
Pastis Mustard? ½ cup mustard seed
1 part vinegar
1 part pastis

no good, too strong

Last July when we were wearing cut-off jeans and stumbling into a liquor store to buy beer for a fireworks party, them farmers out in California's Central Valley were planning our winter for us, dropping seed bombs in the soil to ready the parsnips, squash, beets, hearty greens, and various members of the cauliflower family that they knew we'd be craving right about the time October gets brisk.

While we were camping on rocks in Joshua Tree, eating franks and beans, the farmer dudes' seedlings took root. During our late summer trip to Portland to drink American whiskey with our blogger friends, those seeds sprouted flowers. And once we were back working long weekday nights during the howls of LA's Santa Ana gusts, they were grow-ing heavy with fruit explosions.

That's how flighty summer fun begets our favorite, serious food seasons: win-ter and fall. (If you're saying to yourself, "but Los Angeles doesn't have seasons," shush: we see hard rains in spring, scorching Indian summers, and longer shadows cast by our bicycles—we've even had to wear a sweater in January.)

This is why it's in fall and winter that we send our salad spinners into over-drive. Not like big-bowls-of-romaine salad. Like vegetables-cooked-perfectly salad. Week-long fermented salads and savory breads oozing with herbs and mushrooms count too, of course. Any fresh veg that doesn't take the back seat to rice, noodles, and cheese fries we consider salad. And for that, winter's by far the best.

Cold season produce is a world unto itself, endless to explore, unparalleled in challenge, and impossibly pleasur-able. Whereas summer vegetables are easy—sprinkle them with salt, a little oil, and be done—with winter vegetables you must *try*. They must be cuddled, dressed up, told that they're pretty, and unfolded using fire, steam, vinegar, and butter (as well as those funny tools you get for Christmas). Really, it's like winter itself: harder to survive, something to work through, but reviving all the same.

The book in your greasy digits is a milestone for yours trulies. What started as us poaching an egg in Pabst late one night has led to food truck stints, radio interviews, catering gigs for hundred-guest weddings, and even (gross) TV pitch meetings at ass-hat talent agen-cies. But today we're still nerds who just wanna work on our kitchen tricks in dirty cut-offs while drinking lukewarm twelve-percent-alcohol ales—and try to find some time to write about the new and fucked up things we've con-jured up to do with vegetables. Prime your gullets, say a prayer, and celebrate our Sabbath with us.

♥

a+e

ON THE IMPORTANCE OF

MONGERING

SALT, LIPIDS, CHEESE, SPICE & VINEGAR

While we totally get that not everything needs—or can be affordably topped with—a splash of a $50 Portuguese olive oil, or sea salt granules that've been hand-smoked over some Nordic dude's dismantled ancestral home, sometimes your vegetables deserve it. Ingredients can make or break cooking, and it's doubly true when you're working with lettuces, roasted roots, and braised bulbs. You've heard the old maxim, "Don't cook with wine you wouldn't drink," right? It applies for spices, oils, vinegars, and cheeses too: if you ain't lickin' it off your digits before you toss it in a recipe, you won't be doing so after it's cooked.

The good news is sourcing these fancy frills is fun and painless. Now more than ever before, Americans are giving a shit about what we put in our bodies, and our vast land has become a veritable playground of ingredient superiority.

When we're cooking at home, and for the purposes of this book, farmers market produce is undeniably the star, but the dressings, sauces, and spices in your pantry all work like the backing band. This slick of good oil, that splash of barrel-aged vinegar, a pat of insane Vermont farmstead butter: sometimes these are purely nonnegotiable. Follow these three simple rules and you'll soon be buying the good shit.

1.
You get what you pay for.

When it comes to quality produce, pantry items, good cheese, etc., you must pay to play. Food and booze ought to be your two highest expenditures (after rent and before children).

2.
Enjoy the hunt.

Make shopping more complicated and you'll get better stuff. Find a restaurant-grade specialty store; seek out the best ethnic markets in your city; buy cheese at a cheesestore, beer at a beerstore, and beans directly from a coffee roaster. Most importantly, tap your farmers markets for everything else (find one to be your main market, and one on a different day as backup). Bottom line: the convenience of one-stop shopping is a veiled dagger, ready to bleed the creativity and vitality out of your kitchen.

3.
Find like-minded mongers.

The easiest way to facilitate the full expression of the first two rules is to engage in a relationship with the people you spend money with. If they're not psyched about what they sell, they can go to hell! Many people who work at farmers markets, specialty stores, and bottle shops are in love—love!—with their goods. If you ask their advice or take time to talk shop, you'll reap endless rewards (in the form of tips, trades, and them "forgetting" to put that special edition bottle you asked about on the shelf and plopping it into your hands when you come in). Being able to trust your source is priceless.

Table of Elements

Stop looking for appetizers or soups—tables of contents blow! Here's a non-linear trip through the farmers market, your fridge, and this book.

We don't know about you but when we're shopping at the market we rarely start with a cookbook recipe and go from there. We prefer letting meals reveal themselves to us. We grab what looks good and go home. So pick an ingredient from the table below and check out the possibilities.

Apple **Ap** 79, 85, 106							
Orange **Og** 19, 53, 105	Almond **Am** 34, 88						
Blood Orange **Bo** 38, 116	Cashew **Cw** 34, 54						
Banana **Bn** 105	Peanut **Pn** 34, 113	King Oyster Mushroom **Km** 29, 111	Carrot **Ca** 20, 31, 72, 78	Kohlrabi **Kh** 81	Onion **On** 19, 97	Sweet Potato **Sw** 84	
Grape **Gp** 48, 79, 86	Pecan **Pc** 34, 88, 118	Oyster Mushroom **Om** 29, 30, 100	Celeriac **Cr** 50	Ginger **Gn** 35, 45	Parsnip **Ps** 21, 22, 54, 100	Sunchoke **Su** 77, 79	
Pear **Pe** 116	Black-eyed Pea **Bp** 114	Portobello Mushroom **Pm** 29, 99	Fennel **Fn** 58, 62, 74	Fingerling Potato **Fp** 40, 64	Peruvian Potato **Pv** 27, 82	Shallot **Sh** 45, 56	
Persimmon **Pr** 76	Cranberry **Cb** 49, 51, 53						

Converting to Metric

TEMPERATURE

To convert from Fahrenheit to Celsius, subtract 32 and multiple by .56.

212° F = 100° C
225° F = 110° C
250° F = 120° C
275° F = 135° C
300° F = 150° C
350° F = 180° C
375° F = 190° C
400° F = 200° C
425° F = 220° C

HOT KNIVES | SALAD DAZE

fig A.

Ingredient ——— Apple

Ap

Page Numbers ——— **15, 22, 74**

- page 79, *Pickled Apples*
- page 85, *Apple Soup*
- page 106, *Beer Candied Apples*

Arugula **Ag** 18, 66, 67, 101

Broccoli **Bc** 43, 48, 113	Endive **Ed** 58	Green Tomato **Gt** 85	Okra **Ok** 79, 82	Mustard Green **Mg** 91
Brussels Sprouts **Bs** 51	Delicata Squash **Ds** 88	Green Bean **Gb** 64	Poblano Pepper **Pp** 49, 114	Napa Cabage **Nc** 20

Rosemary **Rs** 34	Dill **Di** 55, 56	Butternut Squash **Bq** 48, 118	Chipotle Pepper **Cp** 82, 92	Kabocha Squash **Ks** 82	Pumpkin **Pk** 87	Radiccio **Rd** 38
Sage **Sg** 36, 88	Thyme **Ty** 58, 64	Lavendar **Lv** 65	Cauliflower **Cf** 22, 43	Fresno Chilie **Fc** 20, 24, 49	Spaghetti Squash **Ss** 36	Kale **Ka** 40, 112
Beet **Bt** 80, 82, 89, 111	Booze **Bz** 35, 44, 53, 91	Buttermilk **Bm** 62	Cheese **Ch** 68, 91, 97	Egg **Eg** 22	Vanilla **Va** 63, 116	Spinach **Sp** 36

LIQUID VOLUME
1 teaspoon = 5 milliliters (ml)
1 tablespoon = 15 ml
1 cup = 240 ml
1 quart = .95 liters (l)
1 gallon = 3.8 l

WEIGHT
1 ounce = 28 grams
1 pound (lb) = .45 kilograms (kg)
2.2 lbs = 1 kg

LENGTH
1/4 inch (in) = .6 centimeters (cm)
1/2 in = 1.25 cm
1 in = 2.5 cm

Citrus y Cebollas

Serves two

It's both thrilling and bizarre that in LA—the birthplace of the burger—one of our most pervasive street foods consists of a plastic bag brimming with fruit, splatted with citrus, and sprinkled with salt. If you're on the right side of the La Brea Avenue dividing line, dudes on every other corner hawk these rugged, street-smart fruit salads. Our twist on this is like a land bridge from Lala Land to Spain—where onions and oranges play frequently, often in the company of olive oil and salt. A little pedestal of chèvre absorbs the extra juice (the little you can stand to not slurp from the salad bowl like some dorm-room guzzler), making for a savory creamsicle vibe that we liberally shower with pomegranate seeds for a fall salad, perfect for when you're pining after summer.

4 ounces fresh chèvre
½ white onion
1 ripe orange
¼ cup pomegranate seeds
1 tablespoon olive oil
¼ cup bitter greens (arugula or frisée)
1 teaspoon unseasoned rice wine vinegar
Maldon sea salt and black pepper to taste

1. Divide the chèvre into two equal portions and roll into balls. Lay two sheets of plastic wrap side by side on a clean flat surface and place each ball in the center of each sheet. Cover the balls with another centered piece of plastic wrap. Using a rolling pin or a pint glass, carefully roll out the cheese until it is about a millimeter thick. Place each flat disk on a plate or other flat surface and stick in your freezer.

2. Cut the onion in half lengthwise, peel away and discard the first two layers. Slice the onion in a thin julienne (a quarter inch thick) and submerge in a bowl filled with cool water. Break up the pieces so they're all individual like.

3. Supreme the orange over a mixing bowl, making sure to reserve every drop of juice. When you've cut out all the segments, give what's left a good squeeze.

4. Seed the pomegranate and wash your greens.

5. Strain the onions and add them to bowl of orange segments and juice; add the pomegranate seeds as well. Add the oil and vinegar and mix with your hands until the juice and the oil have generally incorporated into each other and have covered the fruit.

Throw in the greens and make sure they get sauced.

6. Remove your frozen chèvre from the freezer and discard the top layer of plastic wrap. Using a cookie cutter or a thin-rimmed glass, punch out a shape that you like. Make sure to work gently (the cheese can shatter) and quick (the cheese is harder to handle when warm).

7. Center chèvre plaquettes on two plates and arrange first greens, then onions, oranges, and seeds. Dress the whole mess up with an extra spoon of the vinaigrette-juice and garnish liberally with Maldon salt and fresh ground pepper.

TIP Don't manhandle the pomegranate! Using your knife, carve an "x" into the stem and the base. Use this as an entry point to pry open the fruit along a natural tear, rather than slicing through seeds. Carefully loosen seeds over a bowl of water and then pick through to remove the white stuff. For the orange, peel it whole and then pretend you're slicing up a breakfast grapefruit by running a paring knife between pith to get pristine fruit slices.

Beverage
Jolly Pumpkin
Oro de
Calabaza

Soundtrack
Os Mutantes
"Baby"

Ve
VEGAN

Kimchi

Makes a ton

While Korean cuisine may be the new "it" food in America, we're obsessed with it for the same reason that Koreans are: it fucking rules. Seriously, what's not to love? Hot chiles, fried eggs everywhere, and loads upon loads of fermented vegetables, namely the über pre-choucroute: kimchi. This recipe makes a good amount, and because we use a relatively mild red chile, you can use it liberally and avoid a trip to the store for other flavor enhancers. When it's done, you'll find yourself working this funky-spicy-crunchy wunderkind into just about everything you make. It's great in stews, pulsed into sauces (particularly amazing with veganaise), spread on sandwiches—and you can even take the extra juice and stock base from brine leftovers and make a vinaigrette. Try this once, and then go ape-shit improvising with other wintery veggies.

TIP This'll take you a full eight days to complete: twenty-four hours to brine and at least seven days to ferment. You'll need a large container—we use ceramic crocks. For best results, ferment the veggies in a container, without a lid, placed inside a larger vessel and then cover all of the above with a clean kitchen towel. As for brine, do not use iodized salt or any salt that has anticaking ingredients. Figure out all these elements before you start chopping.

VEGETABLES
1 large Chinese (Napa) cabbage (2–3 pounds)
4 baby bok choy
4 carrots
1 medium daikon radish
2 bunches of scallions

MARINADE PASTE
1 medium-sized ginger bulb (½ pound)
8 Fresno chiles
6 garlic cloves
2–4 medium-sized shallots
1 tablespoon ground gochugaru pepper (Aleppo pepper also works)

BRINE
6 quarts water
2 cups kosher salt

Beverage

Oskar Blues
GUBNA
Imperial IPA

Soundtrack

Talisman
*Initiate into
the Mysteries*

1. Prep the veg: peel the daikon and carrots. Slice the carrots in half lengthwise and cut a quarter inch thick on a bias. Keep the daikon whole but slice similarly thin. Remove outer two to three layers of the Napa cabbage and discard, then break the remaining leaves off by hand, keeping them whole. Peel off all the leaves from each of the baby bok choy, trimming the ends that attach to the stem. Trim the scallions, keeping only the white, peeling off outermost skin. Wash all veg and dry in a salad spinner.

2. Toss all of these veggies into your aging vessel. In a separate container, mix the salt with the water until dissolved.

3. Dump the salt brine over the veggies and mix around with your (clean) hands. Your veggies need not be completely submerged in brine, but your container should be at least three-quarters full of liquid. Place a clean plate, or brine-filled plastic bag, on top of the whole mess and weigh it down with a heavy sterile object (a jar filled with water works). Press down a little and soon the pressure of the weighted plate will cause the veggies to release some of their liquids, which will comingle with the brine and immerse what we call the "pre-chi." Cover the container with a towel and let ferment at room temperature for twenty-four hours.

4. Prepare the paste: peel the ginger with a spoon and grate with the smallest hole on a box grater; set aside (reserve peel for stock). Roughly chop the chiles, shallots, and garlic. Puree all the ginger, scallion tips, garlic, shallots, and chiles in a food processor or blender for several minutes. Add a tablespoon or two of brine to help the mixture move. Place the paste in a jar and mix in gochugaru, Aleppo, or any other red chile pepper flakes. Seal the lid and let ferment on your counter overnight.

· · · · · · · · 24 Hours Later · · · · · · ·

5. Drain the brine off of the veggies (reserve brine in the fridge indefinitely). Taste the veggies. They should be salty but not unpleasantly so. If they're too salty, rinse them in cold water and taste again.

6. Mix the flavor paste and the veggies and cram the whole mess back into the aging vessel, pressing the veggies down. Compacting them will release the juices they need to preserve themselves properly. Place the vessel inside a larger container and cover again with a towel and ferment for seven days. They are ready when they taste almost effervescent: spicy, funky, forever.

Bibimbop

Serves two

One of the first times we made our version of this Korean tofu-house staple, we nearly over-dosed on the word "bibimbop," never wanting to utter it again. A few winters ago, we staged a film shoot of us cooking with some friends for a fun little TV pilot. As a hint of (wicked) things to come, an actual reality television producer tagged along to give us some pointers and provocations. This ass-kisser of a hanger-on had two things in mind for Hot Knives: we had to show we were a) food snob assholes and b) closeted gay lovers locked in a sordid kitchen bromance (Bravo channel would love this, she said). Never mind that this was not the show we had in mind, our producer had us repeating "bibimbop" like it was a hiccup and slapping each other on the back while we cooked until we nearly lost the courage of our convictions—and our appetite. Needless to say, TV didn't work out. But the bibimbop sure did!

1 parsnip
½ head cauliflower
½ head green or yellow cauliflower
1 small ginger bulb
1 ½ tablespoon grapeseed oil
1 teaspoon rice wine vinegar
1 teaspoon Mirin rice wine
½ teaspoon olive oil
1 teaspoon soy sauce
1 sprig cilantro
½ cup kimchi
2 organic eggs
Sea salt and pepper to taste

Beverage

Russian River
Blind Pig IPA

Soundtrack

Girls' Generation
"Gee"

1. "Rice" the veggies starting with the two cauliflowers. Snap off the outer most florets and slice each one lengthwise into four or five long pieces. Turn ninety degrees and slice again, but only three lengthwise cuts. Finally slip to cut from the base to the top, leaving you with a somewhat rice kernel–sized dice. Repeat until you have about two cups or more.

2. Peel and dice the ginger and parsnip. In a small bowl, combine the rice wine vinegar, Mirin rice wine, olive oil, and soy. Stir and set aside.

3. Heat a skillet on medium heat and add a tablespoon of grapeseed oil. Once hot, add the riced veggies and ginger. Stir with a wooden spoon every thirty seconds or so to keep from sticking. Cook this way until veggies cook down and start to brown, then add liquid and cook for another minute before removing and dishing into two bowls, keeping them warm on the stove.

4. Grease a clean skillet on high heat with more grapeseed oil and fry your eggs, cooking just under over-medium. Salt and pepper after flipping. Plate the eggs and return the cast-iron to high heat; add kimchi and cook just until thoroughly hot. Add to the plate along with cilantro leaves for garnish.

Cock Sauce

Makes 2 cups

We first attempted our own concoction of this infamous, sweet hot sauce in the green-top squeeze bottle when the manufacturer hit a supply-and-demand snag a few years ago. Their local factory was behind on orders and restaurants as far as Dallas, Texas, were starting to call LA food distributors looking for a fix. When we got word of the shortage, we freaked, terrified of running out ourselves. So we improvised a quick, fresh nuclear orange puree that we thought came pretty close. In retrospect, we were kidding ourselves. That sweet tang is not just sugar (although there's that, too). The real thang is aged for several days to let the chile and garlic ferment until bubbly. With that secret in our hands, our Cock Sauce finally went head to... erm... head, with the real stuff.

12 red Fresno chiles (about a pound)
3–4 cloves garlic
4 tablespoons filtered water
2 teaspoons kosher salt
¼ cup sugar
¼ cup distilled white vinegar
⅛ cup rice wine vinegar

1. Remove stems from your chiles and roughly chop 'em up. Toss them in your blender or food processor (seeds and all). Peel and add garlic. Combine salt and water in a small bowl and stir to dissolve.

2. Pulse the mixture for about a minute, adding the salted water to help it move. Add more as needed.

3. Transfer the mixture into a glass vessel using a spatula and cover it tightly with plastic wrap. Set aside somewhere warm and let ferment for four days.

· · · · · · · · · *4 Days Later* · · · · · · · ·

4. Remove plastic and skim any discolored spots. Dump the fermented chile paste into a sauce pot and place on medium heat. Add vinegars and sugar. Let the mixture hit a rolling boil, stir it, and turn down to simmer. Let cook for five minutes before turning off and letting it cool.

5. Return the mixture to a food processor and blend thoroughly one last time, about two minutes, or until the seeds are completely crushed and you've attained a beautiful, fiery red-orange sauce.

6. Place a fine mesh strainer over a clean storage vessel and dump the puree into the strainer. Using a spatula, gently press the puree to filter it through the mesh. Once you're left with just a goopy pile of crushed fiber in the strainer, discard it and you're done. Bottle cock sauce and use as desired.

Beverage

Uehara Shuzou
Echigo Stout

Soundtrack

The Make-Up
"I Am If..."

HOT KNIVES | SALAD DAZE

25

fleur de sel

SALT

gris

The most essential ingredient in this book is also the simplest to explain. Salt is like air: without it, you die. Literally. And yet salt, like the ever-shunned carb, was a one-time devil that many people told you to avoid. These people are now all dead (to us).

If you can afford not to, never use mechanically evaporated salt. What's the price difference between French sea salt hand harvested from ancient salt marshes then dried by the sun and some crappy-ass boiling project funded by CarGill? About three dollars. If you can't part with the extra bucks for real-deal sea salt, the next best buy is kosher salt, which we keep a cereal box-sized carton of for cooking and pickling purposes.

When you go any cheaper, read the ingredients. Seriously! Even some large-scale sea salt concerns add anticaking agents, dyes, and other unpronounceable chemicals. Any of that shit will ruin your pickling efforts. Don't let Big Salt get away with spoiling your kimchi or dill spears.

When you splurge, resist the temptation to dash novelty salts like truffle salt or the prissy volcanic Hawaiian shit into a vat of pasta water. The more expensive the granules of sodium, the closer to your mouth you want to keep them. Use the most unrefined sea salt you can find for seasoning soups, sauces, batters, and dressings (French sel gris de Guerande is the ticket); and save the fancier granules like fleur de sel or Maldon for finishing.

smoked

When you use salt, use it wisely—which is not the same as sparsely. Think about the application, consider what else is on the plate, taste the sauce, and know your preference. We go heavy because vegetables taste better that way. When we say "pinch" in a recipe we probably squeezed in two.

Maldon

Hot Chips

Serves four

There's nothing wrong with potato chips in a bag. Except their temperature: they are cold. Science has proven chips—like anything fried—are better hot. We like to use a mix of purple Peruvian and something paler—either Yukon Gold or something more farmers market-friendly, like long, nondescript red-skinned beauties. We sit the potatoes in water overnight to strip them of their stickiest starches and finish them the next day in a cast-iron pot filled with canola oil bubbling on the stove.

> 4 medium potatoes
> ½ gallon canola oil
> 1 tablespoon sea salt
> 1 tablespoon Aleppo pepper
> 1 tablespoon minced flat leaf parsley

1. Scrub potatoes clean and slice them using a mandolin to achieve a consistent paper-thin quality. If you slice them lengthwise, you'll get nice long chips.

2. To rinse 'em, fill two large containers (stock pots work well) half way with clean water. Fill one with sliced potatoes and swirl them around/scrub them against each other to get rid of excess starch. After a few minutes of this, transfer the partially clean potatoes into the other pot of clear water and repeat, replacing the starchy water with clean, until the chips are not releasing any starch.

3. Place the now clean potato slices in a large Tupperware and cover with fresh water. Sit in the fridge overnight.

· · · · · · · · *24 Hours Later* · · · · · · · ·

4. Pick a large vessel appropriate for the size batch you're making (a cast-iron pot or your favorite, sturdy soup pot) and fill at least half full with canola oil. Keep on high heat for about twenty minutes, until oil is hot, hot, hot! Don't bother with a thermometer—drop in one dry chip to test. It should float and sizzle hard.

5. Vigorously dry the chips using a salad spinner until they are hardly damp at all. Pat them dry and let sit if need be.

6. Drop chips in small handfuls, never exceeding a ratio of roughly one-fifth chips to four-fifths oil. Once the first chips start to brown, fish them out with a spider strainer or tongs. Drip dry on paper towels.

6. Season with salt, Aleppo pepper, and parsley, and serve.

Beverage

Lagunitas Hop Stoopid Ale

Soundtrack

Hot Chip "Ready For the Floor"

TIP At a backyard barbecue stand we ran one summer, we found out the hard way that dropping too many potatoes can cause oil eruption spill-overs and ensuing grease fires. The best advice we can give you? Start with a very small handful at first and don't do this barefoot.

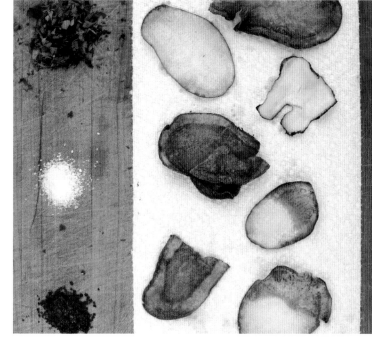

Cast-Iron Mushrooms

Makes 3–4 cups

The next best thing to foraging your own wild mushrooms and huffing their death-matter musk from a Hobbitshire-like hillside in NorCal while your guide trips on psilocybin shrooms is (obviously) slurping crispy hot shrooms right out of the cast-iron skillet they were cooked in. Admittedly, it's a distant second. But it still feels nasty. Thanks to the whole steak joint steeze revival, it's now totally acceptable to eat out of cast-iron. Here we do a mushroom mélange of various shapes, sizes, textures, and prices. Omit and add as you like, especially if you actually get to forage for wild ones.

½ pound crimini mushrooms
½ pound white button mushrooms
½ pound oyster mushrooms
2 king oyster mushrooms
1 portobello mushroom
2 shallots, sliced paper thin
1 tablespoon butter or margarine
2 cloves garlic, minced
2 tablespoons parsley, chopped
sea salt and pepper to taste

1. Place your trusty cast-iron skillet in the middle of your oven and preheat to 500 degrees. This will take thirty minutes.

2. Prepare the mushrooms. With a damp towel wipe off any dirt. If you must rinse them, do so gently and pat dry.

3. Create various shroom shapes. Slice crimini and button mushrooms in half. Remove the bottom tuft of the king oyster mushrooms and discard, then slice lengthwise into four or five long pieces before cutting down the middle so you have short rectangles. Rip the oyster mushrooms into halves by hand. Slice the portobello into quarters or eighths as desired.

4. Remove the pan and add all the mushrooms. Return it to the oven for five minutes. Then remove again, and stir the shrooms so that any sides unexposed to the hot iron can't help getting a good sear. Cook for an additional five minutes.

5. Remove the pan and add the shallots, butter, and toss. Return to the oven for another five minutes.

6. Final removal: add the garlic and parsley. Let sizzle in front of your drooling friends for three to five minutes. Salt generously, pepper profusely, and signal the attack.

Beverage

Avery The Kaiser
Imperial
Oktoberfest Lager

Soundtrack

Shit Robot
"Simple Things"

VEGAN

Veggie Stock

Makes 8 cups

With any luck, you now have a large stinking mass of fermenting cabbage, chiles, and onions hanging out in your house, scaring your kids, making your lover a little less interested in getting naked, fascinating your cats, etc. If you've been good, you also have a large amount of brine leftover from an initial kimchi, kraut, or pickling freakfest. This brine, with a little love, can turn into your own personal solution to any cold front, head cold, or cold war: simple and awesome stock. This is not something that will take you all day and you can—you will—use it in many other applications in this book (and whenever you need to swap spit for chicken stock in all the other cookbooks you'll soon never open again).

2 cups brine
6 cups filtered water
1 onion
1 tablespoon grapeseed oil
3 cups assorted winter vegetable trimmings

BEVERAGE

Port Midnight
Sessions Lager

SOUNDTRACK

Althea and Donna
"Upton Top Ranking"

1. Heat a large pot on high, greased with oil. Chop your onion, skin on, any way you like.

2. Sauté the onion, and any trimmings you have on hand—carrot peels, tomato tops, potato skins, whatever—until some nice browning begins. Remember: color is flavor.

3. Add the brine and the water at room temperature. Cook on medium heat until boiling steadily. Cook for an additional forty-five minutes to an hour. Strain, season, and use.

VEGAN

Magic Shroom Dust

Makes 1 cup

If there's one "gateway meat" that seems to lure plant eaters back into the blood, it's pork—specifically bacon: sweet, salty, smoky, sumptuous bacon. But behind every pig's butt there is delicious produce, whether it's acorns or grass, fungi or nuts. That's what the smart critters like. So, we figure, why not go straight to the source and cultivate a sweet, salty—even fatty—plant matter? Rather than rely on the soy and food coloring that makes Bacos what they are, we picked up some oyster mushrooms and pepitas at our farmers market and stumbled upon a deeply oily crumble that rules on salads, dips, fried eggs—anything but pork belly.

1 pound oyster mushrooms
2 cups raw pepitas
1 tablespoon olive oil
1 tablespoon smoked salt
1 teaspoon smoked paprika
1 teaspoon black pepper
1 teaspoon maple syrup
canola spray

BEVERAGE

Goose Island
Bourbon
County Stout

SOUNDTRACK

Umberto
"Someone Chasing
Someone through
a House"

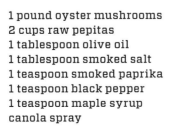

1. Preheat the oven to 375 degrees. Tear the oyster mushrooms into long lengthwise shreds, so that each piece runs from mushroom cap to the woodier stem, and place in a mixing bowl.

2. Toss the mushrooms with olive oil, smoked salt, black pepper, paprika, and maple syrup. Spray a baking sheet lightly with canola oil and lay mushrooms out evenly, then spray the mushrooms as well. Cook in the oven for ten to twelve minutes or until brown and crispy.

3. In a large skillet, toast the pepitas on medium-high heat, tossing every couple minutes to cook evenly. Remove from heat.

4. Cool both mushrooms and pepitas to room temperature. Combine and pulse in a food processor in several quick cycles. You want a fine crumb consistency.

5. Return to baking sheet, evenly distributed and sprayed with canola oil, and put in oven for another five to ten minutes, or until dry. Store the cool, dry, crumbs in the fridge.

Daikon Stew

Serves four

You can measure the temperature in LA by looking in our fridge: if there's more than one daikon, it's cold and stormy. That's probably cuz this long, unwieldy white radish is one of our favorite things to cook in winter weather. Seared and braised these suckers turn into sauce sponges. At the root of a simple stew, it's one of the best ways we know to take the chill out of our Angelino bones.

> 1 tablespoon grapeseed oil
> 1 large daikon radish
> 2 large carrots
> 5 scallions
> 3 cloves garlic
> 1 tablespoon soy sauce
> 1 tablespoon rice wine vinegar
> 4 sprigs cilantro
> 8 cups veggie stock
> 1 cup Cast-Iron Mushrooms (pg. 28)
> 1 cup kimchi (optional)

1. Skin and then slice the daikon into ¼-inch thick silver dollars. Skin and then cut the carrot similarly, on a forty-five–degree bias. Trim and mince the scallions and the garlic.

2. Heat the grapeseed oil in a large pot on high heat. Once hot, place the daikon rounds face down onto the hot oiled surface. Sear for forty-five seconds and then add the carrots, garlic, and scallions—but do not stir.

3. Add the braising liquid: dump in soy sauce and rice vinegar and let cook off for two full minutes. Then add your cooked mushrooms and the stock. Now you can stir. Bring the pot to a boil, then simmer until the daikon is cooked through, about fifteen to twenty minutes.

4. If you are adding kimchi, give it a rough chop first, then toss it and cilantro into the bottom of each diner's bowl, and finally top it all off with boiling hot soup.

BEVERAGE

McEwan's
Scotch Ale

SOUNDTRACK

Sister Nancy
"Gwan a School"

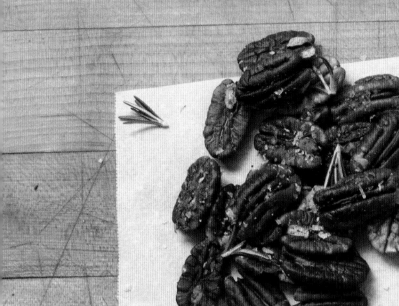

SAVORY PECANS

Hot Nuts

SPICY PEANUTS

SMOKEY ALMONDS

Protein + fat = snack attack. Buying raw and roasting at home beats store-bought snacks anyday.

SWEETER CASHEWS

1. Melt butter or margarine in a double boiler; if using butter, skim off white foam to clarify. Combine the primary spices with the clarified butter and let sit for several minutes while you preheat oven to 300 degrees (save salt and pepper for garnish).

2. Toss the nuts in your spiced or sweetened fat (depending on recipe) and distribute evenly.

3. Lay nuts on a greased baking sheet and cook in the oven for twenty to thirty minutes or until they start to slightly brown, being careful not to burn them.

4. Let cool for at least ten minutes to allow nuts to crisp. Add sea salt or fresh cracked pepper to taste.

1. For the peanut recipe, combine herbs and spices with oil in a sauce pan and simmer for ten to fifteen minutes. Set aside to cool while you preheat the oven to 325 degrees.

2. Strain the herbs and spices out of the oil. Toss the nuts with your flavored oil in a bowl, coating evenly.

3. Lay nuts on a greased baking sheet and cook for about twenty minutes or until they start to slightly brown. Let cool for at least ten minutes before eating to allow nuts to crisp.

4. Salt and garnish with chopped cilantro and another minced red chile for garnish.

Sweeter Cashews

1 cup cashews
3 tablespoon butter or margarine
1 vanilla pod, split and scraped
2 tablespoons honey (agave works)
1 teaspoon sea salt

Savory Pecans

1 cup pecans
3 tablespoons butter or margarine
2 teaspoons fresh rosemary, finely chopped
1 teaspoon black pepper
1 teaspoon sea salt
1 teaspoon additional chopped rosemary for garnish

Smokey Almonds

1 cup raw almonds
3 tablespoons butter or margarine
2 teaspoons smoked paprika
1 teaspoon smoked salt
1 ½ teaspoon Urfa biber (optional)
1 teaspoon additional smoked paprika for garnish
1 teaspoon sea salt

Spicy Peanuts

1 cup peanuts
4 tablespoons grapeseed or canola oil
1 stalk lemongrass
1 teaspoon minced shallot
2 cloves garlic
1 Thai red chile
½ teaspoon turmeric
½ teaspoon fresh coriander seeds
1 teaspoon sea salt
1 tablespoon fresh cilantro

KniQuil

Makes three doses

When we made this medicine-booze concoction on a live NPR radio affiliate last year, our gracious host immediately confided in us that, yes, she too had been addicted to the Green Dragon. Working in restaurants as a young line cook, she apparently liked to fill coffee mugs with NyQuil and chug it throughout the night. We thought that was the most insane thing we'd ever heard. But since then, more and more people have told us similar stories. It's a good thing we developed a natural version of the hard stuff. You can skip the drugs and take on the flu with fresh produce, organic sweeteners, and thimbles of liquor instead. Our recipe replaces pain-and-fever-reliever acetaminophen, cough suppressant dextromethorphan HBr, and sleep aid doxylamine succinate with roasted green chiles, ginger, citric acid, and booze—all-natural forms of the chemical stuff. Throw on some sweatpants, get cozy on the couch, and take a couple shots—er, doses—of this concoction to wage war on your symptoms. Take that Big Pharma!

- 2 cups fresh mint leaves
- 1 cup agave (or honey)
- 1 lemon
- 1 teaspoon olive oil
- 1 tablespoon fresh ginger
- 1 tablespoon roasted green chile
- 1 shot pastis
- 1 shot whiskey

1. In a saucepan, bring 1 cup roughly chopped fresh mint leaves and 1 cup water to a boil. Simmer for five minutes then strain out the leaves. Bring just the mint water back to a boil over medium heat. Whisk in the agave nectar or honey, boil one more minute, and let cool.

2. In a small dish, combine the zest of the lemon with olive oil and set aside.

3. In a blender, combine grated fresh ginger, roasted green chiles, and the remaining fresh mint leaves. Add the lemon juice and half the mint syrup; pulse thoroughly. Pass the mixture through a mesh strainer, stirring with a spoon to help it along. Taste the juice; if it seems too tart or spicy, add more mint syrup.

4. To create a dose of your homemade medicine, combine 1 tablespoon of this juice with 1 tablespoon each of pastis and whiskey in a cocktail shaker. Add 1 teaspoon of the lemon-zest oil, several ice cubes, and shake. Pour into a shot glass and drink up.

BEVERAGE

Craftsman
Aurora Borealis

SOUNDTRACK

EC8OR
"Gimme NyQuil
All Night Long"

Squash Noodles, Sage Pesto

Serves four

Your freezer is for ice cubes, booze, and batteries—not herbs. Don't convince yourself it's okay to freeze your fresh basil pesto. Unless you have a hot-house hook-up, we recommend you forgo summer pesto for a winter one when fresh basil goes away for the winter—how's that go? Love the one you're with? This spread of spinach, hazelnuts, and sage is deep and woodsy, somewhere between pesto and stuffing, ideal slathered on roasted spaghetti squash "noodles." Not only does the canary-yellow poke through the emerald green pesto in a way that noodles can't, there's something devilish about a vegetable masquerading as a carb.

SAGE PESTO
1 cup fresh spinach
½ cup hazelnuts
½ cup olive oil
2 cloves garlic
6–8 fresh sage leaves
½ teaspoon fresh grated nutmeg
sea salt and pepper to taste

SQUASH "NOODLES"
1 spaghetti squash
canola spray
1 tablespoon olive oil
extra veg as desired
sea salt to taste

1. First toast the hazelnuts in a pan (be careful not to burn them) and let cool for at least twenty minutes. Then combine spinach, hazelnuts, garlic, and half the olive oil in a food processor and pulse while slowly drizzling in the remaining oil. Stop pulsing to add the sage leaves and nutmeg; salt to taste. Finish by pulsing for another ten seconds. Remove and set aside.

2. Preheat the oven to 325 degrees and spray a baking sheet with canola oil. Break down the squash by splitting it down the middle, discarding the seeds and slicing it into eight to ten segments. Make sure to cut with the grain of the squash: there should be an identifiable direction the groove of the flesh runs, and your "noodles" will be less noodly if you cut across the grain and make them too short.

3. Slide the squash onto the pan and into the oven. Cook for about twenty minutes.

4. Remove squash from oven just before it starts to brown. The pieces should break apart easily under pressure. Let cool enough to handle, break each segment apart by hand, collecting the "noodles" in a large bowl.

5. If you want to toss with extra veggies, prepare them now (we like beech mushrooms, cherry tomatoes, and baby spinach).

6. Toss the warm "noodles" in remaining oil and some sea salt, then add any additional veg. Serve in a "bird's nest" shape atop sage pesto and garnish with Italian parsley or baby spinach leaves.

BEVERAGE

The Bruery Mischief

SOUNDTRACK

Stereolab
"Italian Shoes Continuum"

Hot Rad Salad

Serves two

First, know this: there will be bitter. Radicchio is a bitter leaf to swallow, and all the honey in the world won't change that. But we have a way to tame this red veiny lettuce that's sometimes nicknamed Italian chicory. Available perennially from your local leaf-slinger, radicchio makes for easy grilling and can add a colorful punch to raw salads. In cold months, we prefer to pan-roast the torn leaves with a sweet and savory dressing that coaxes out their Italian roots without being heavy-handed: toasted fennel seeds, red chiles, and citrusy olive oil. Think of this as pizza in a bowl.

    1 large head radicchio
    1 blood orange
    1 tablespoon extra virgin olive oil
    1 teaspoon fennel seeds
    1 red Fresno chile
    1 small carrot
    ½ white onion
    6-8 ounces Winter Seitan (pg. 70)
    1 tablespoon cornmeal
    1 tablespoon grapeseed oil
    1 tablespoon whole grain mustard
    ⅛ cup red wine
    1 teaspoon cider vinegar
    1 teaspoon sugar (honey works too)

BEVERAGE

Pretty Things Saint Botolph's Town Rustic Dark Ale

SOUNDTRACK

The xx
"Hot Like Fire"

1. Quarter and core your radicchio. Peel the leaves off one at a time and place in a mixing bowl. Zest and then juice the orange and sit zest in olive oil for a few minutes, and add fennel seeds to the juice. Dump both mixtures onto the radicchio leaves and stir well with tongs.

2. Slice your onion and Fresno pepper into half-moons and matchsticks respectively. Mix together mustard, wine, sugar, and vinegar. Add a teaspoon of water and stir. Marinate the onion and pepper sticks in this dressing.

3. Slice the seitan into neat, right triangles about an inch long. Fill a large plate with cornmeal and pat the seitan with a cornmeal crust. Heat a large skillet on high heat, add grapeseed oil, then drop in seitan. Cook evenly on both sides for several minutes and remove seitan from pan, resting on a plate.

4. Still on high heat, add the marinated radicchio to the skillet and stir, followed by the marinating onions and dressing. Stir every so often for four to five minutes, letting the radicchio cook down (it should wilt like cabbage). Serve on a large plate by twisting the salad into a neat ball, as high as you can. Slice carrot matchsticks and add for garnish and color. Finally, place four or five seitan triangles next to the salad. Garnish with an extra slice of blood orange.

Kale & Potato Breakfast Salad

Serves six

We're guessing the number of Americans who eat McDonald's hashbrowns for breakfast every day would scare us. But we also understand. A hot, perfectly cooked potato with tasty grease and lotsa salt is exactly the kind of carboload that will get you down the road. Knowing this—and also recognizing that we don't want to weigh 300 pounds and be dying with caked arteries—we twist something like hash browns into a good-for-you green salad. In this case, sugars (from the molasses) and salty spice-caked fingerlings get fried, and then handfuls of flavor-sponge kale cooked in wine and grease-drippings follow right behind. We like to think that kale scrubs our arteries clean. Please, scientists, don't conduct a study to prove us wrong.

    2 pounds fingerling potatoes
    2 tablespoons cornmeal
    1 teaspoon kosher salt
    ½ teaspoon paprika
    ½ teaspoon smoked salt
    1 ½ tablespoons olive oil
    2 teaspoon dark molasses
    1 small bunch curly kale
    1 small bunch purple kale
    ¼ cup Madeira wine
    1 shallot, peeled and sliced

1. Prepare the potatoes first. Rinse or scrub off any dirt and cut each fingerling into halves, slicing lengthwise. Throw in a pot of salted water and bring to boil on high heat.

2. While you wait, rip the kale, removing the rib and stem and shredding into large but manageable pieces, then wash and dry. Set aside.

3. As soon as the potato pot hits a rolling boil, remove from heat and let stand for two to three minutes, then drain and cool in cold water. Finally, drain again and let sit to dry. Prepare a spice rub by mixing together cornmeal, paprika, salt, and smoked salt. In a bowl, toss the potatoes with the spices until fully covered.

4. Put a large skillet on medium-high heat and add a tablespoon of olive oil. Once hot, toss potatoes into the pan. Shake the pan firmly every thirty seconds to keep potatoes from sticking. Let cook for several minutes, then slowly add molasses, evenly distributing on potatoes. Continue to cook and shake until some potatoes develop a dark brown caramelized color. Remove potatoes to a bowl and return skillet to high heat without washing.

5. Add remaining oil and sliced shallots to the skillet, stirring and cooking until slightly brown. Add the Madeira wine and wait several seconds before adding all the kale and covering with a lid. Let cook for two to three minutes or until kale has cooked down by half. Salt the kale to taste before plating. Form a bed of kale on each plate topped by several potatoes.

BEVERAGE

Mikkeller Beer
Geek Brunch

SOUNDTRACK

Dinosaur Jr.
"Freak Scene"

SPICES

HOT KNIVES
H✕K
EST. 2005

Unlike beers, cheese, and sexual technique, spices do not improve with time. If you have spices older than your last birthday, use 'em or lose 'em. And if you buy spices from the grocery store, you are getting fleeced by The Man. Do yourself a favor and find a spice shop or mail order from places like Penzeys. As for what to buy, get whole when in doubt, and grind and toast spices yourself. Here are a couple non-powdered gems we insist you keep close to home:

Aleppo Pepper
What: Syrian crushed red pepper
Why: medium heat, pretty red color, earthy tones

Cumin Seed
What: Biblical seed of a flowering Mediterranean plant
Why: rich, beefy tones; smells and tastes like winter

Coriander Seed
What: ubiquitous but oft-hated dry fruit seed
Why: citrus, herb, and soap all in one

Fennel Seed
What: dried, anise-like seed from the flowering bulb
Why: the perfect meat-cheat for sausage flashbacks

Smoked Paprika
What: dried mild chiles smoked over wood, old-school style
Why: stains anything and everything a punishing red and tastes like campfire

Cardamom
What: Indian ginger family seed pod
Why: Christmas and the Far East in a bottle

VEGAN

Blasted Broccoli

Serves four

You read correctly—blasted. We nearly fell from our bar stools one night at a tapas restaurant on the Seattle wharf when a waitress warned us that their broccoli comes charred—because the chef likes to "blast it." We're still puzzled as to what that guy's formal "blasting" technique entailed, but it ruled. His broc was so good that we char-broiled all manner of brassicas until we stumbled upon our own method for "blasting" cabbage-family veggies: once thoroughly dry-charred, we wet the florets with a kimchi puree.

    1 head broccoli
    1 head white cauliflower
    1 head yellow or purple cauliflower
    1 tablespoon grapeseed oil
    1 teaspoon sesame oil
    1 cup kimchi (pg. 20)
    1 teaspoon black sesame seeds

1. Pulse kimchi in a blender. Set aside.

2. Set the oven to 500 degrees. If not already well lubed, rub a tablespoon of oil into your pan. Once the oven's hot, place the pan at the far back, for maximum heat. Heat the pan for about thirty minutes.

3. Wash and dry the broccoli and cauliflower—make sure they're not wet! Break down both by ripping large florets free of their stumpy stem by hand; do not chop. In a large mixing bowl, toss the florets with half the canola oil and all of the sesame oil.

4. Pull your blasting pan toward the front of the oven and add the broccoli and cauliflower. Return to the back. Check and stir every five minutes or so, and cook this way for fifteen to twenty minutes or until some of the florets reveal blackened, frizzled tops.

5. Remove and serve immediately. Spoon several tablespoons of kimchi vinaigrette onto the center of each plate, then stack the hot florets on top in a mixed fashion for color contrast. Sprinkle with sesame seeds and salt to taste.

TIP For proper blasting, you'll need a well-lubed cast-iron pan or Dutch oven. The trick is to create an oven within an oven, so push whatever pan you use to the farthest, hottest spot and let it reach high temp before adding the veggies.

BEVERAGE

Hitachino
Nest XH

SOUNDTRACK

Satan's Pilgrims
"Burnin' Rubber"

HOT KNIVES | SALAD DAZE

Booze-Infused Peppercorns

Makes 2 tablespoons

Like discoveries in other experimental fields, the ones that happen in the kitchen are often rooted in mistakes. When way too many black peppercorns got dumped into hot oil for a pre-bean fry it seemed they were lost. What to do with a pile of soggy, greasy peppercorns? We got to thinking about pepper and what it is: the aged berries from an epic spice tree originating in Indonesia. Black peppercorns are actually sun-cured green peppercorns, and white ones are just black peppercorns that have been soaked, skinned, and dried again. While we didn't follow through with our initial idea to make our own white pepper, we figured we could redry the soggy dudes in a low oven to revive them. The result ruled: the pepper reabsorbed the tasty oil, intensifying its flavor. Ever vigilant in our search for ways to put the liquors we love back into the food we eat, we postulated that we could do the same with booze—bourbon, mescal, pastis, amaro—just about anything. The result is the same; by investing a pony of your favorite sauce, you can elevate the contents of your pepper mill to dizzying heights. You also will make your house smell like a distillery for an hour or two, and your roommates, if you have them, will be wandering around looking for phantom whiskey spills. This technique spikes soups, salads, fresh cheeses, and eggs with that hair-of-the-dog flavor that you've been missing. Booze infusion is the new umami!

BEVERAGE

Lost Abbey
Angels' Share

SOUNDTRACK

Rolling Stones
"Sweet Black Angel"

2 tablespoons whole black peppercorns
2 tablespoons booze of choice (we like whiskey and gin)

1. Heat sauce pot on medium heat and lightly toast the pepper for two to three minutes.

2. Dump in your shot of booze. The liquor should begin cooking off immediately, but you don't want it to burn, so turn the heat as low as possible.

3. When the liquid is completely evaporated and absorbed, turn off the heat. Line a baking sheet with parchment paper (do yourself a favor and buy a roll; it's really indispensable) and spread out the peppercorns evenly.

4. Bake in a low oven, around 250 degrees, for fifteen to twenty minutes. You want the pepper to be completely dry. During the infusion process the peppercorns will swell with liquid and lose their dried look; when they've dried completely they will look exactly like they did before boozin'.

5. Let the peppercorns cool and find something to put them on.

Our Vadouvan

Makes 3–4 cups

Imperialism: while we want to smash it, it bears fruits that we want to rub all over ourselves (and you). This type of curry, vadouvan, is the result of French imperialists' combining the second most essential element of French cuisine—onions—with traditional Indian masala spices. Vadouvan has been popularized by, like, every chef that matters, but few of them actually make their own. Instead, they opt to buy it for $60 a pound wholesale. Ours follows a secret recipe that was pried from the dead hands of a Tamil Tiger's corpse and smuggled into LA with a shipment of something else that we can't mention here. If you want to take this to the next level, go traditional and roll the finished product—a kind of caramelized spice onion mixture—into little balls and dry-ferment them in the sun. Either way, your house will never smell the same again, and you'll find yourself with a curry jerky to add to everything from elegant stews to pans of hot butter.

1 pound shallots, peeled and thinly sliced
2 white onions, peeled and thinly sliced
½ pound ginger, peeled and thinly sliced
2 heads garlic, peeled and thinly sliced
¼ cup grapeseed oil, divided in two
1 tablespoon whole fenugreek
10 whole cloves
2 tablespoons coriander seeds
1 tablespoon cumin seeds

1 ½ teaspoons mustard seeds
1 tablespoon fennel seeds
1 tablespoon red chile flakes
1 tablespoon turmeric powder
1 teaspoon ground nutmeg
1 teaspoon ground cinnamon
30 curry leaves (optional)
1 tablespoon sea salt

1. You will make this in two stages. Heat your trusty cast-iron on a medium flame and add half the grapeseed oil. While it heats, mix the shallots, onions, ginger, and half the garlic in a mixing bowl. When the oil's hot, add half—or close to half—of your mix of ginger, onion, and garlic to the pan. Do not touch it for ten minutes.

2. Now, assemble all your spices except for the chile flakes, nutmeg, cinnamon, and turmeric, and throw them in a separate sauté pan on medium heat. Toss often. When the mustard seeds start to pop (you'll hear it) the spices are toasted. Grind them in your coffee grinder—all the better if it still has some grounds in it—and mix with the chile flakes, nutmeg, cinnamon, and turmeric.

3. Stir your cooking veggies. They should be browning nicely. You want to fully caramelize them but not burn them. After a good stir, leave them alone for another ten minutes.

4. When this mix is getting gently brown, add half, or some approximation thereof, of the spice mix. Julienne the curry leaves (if you can find them) and add to the mix.

5. Line a baking sheet with parchment paper, and turn out your now-caramelized, spicy goo. Spread it as thinly as possible and throw the pan in a cold oven; set it at 250 degrees or "low." You will be drying the vadouvan out—essentially simulating drying it in the sun—for one to three hours. Check it every thirty minutes and spread the onions out as they dry so that there is as thin a layer on the pan as possible. When the mix can be lifted off the pan in sheets, and its color has set a nice blond caramel, you're done!

6. Repeat the process with the rest of your aromatics and spices. Smell success.

BEVERAGE

Avery Maharaja
Imperial IPA

SOUNDTRACK

The Deeep
"Mudd"

Dressings

Vinaigrette is a dress not just for greens—truss up all your veggies with these trusty emulsions and triumph without resorting to anything from a bottle.

SHERRY VINAIGRETTE

Blue Cheese Vinaigrette

1 ounce blue cheese
4 tablespoons crème fraiche (pg. 62)
1 teaspoon filtered water
2 tablespoons apple cider vinegar
1 teaspoon black pepper
sea salt to taste

1. Break apart the blue cheese in a bowl. Add crème fraiche, water, vinegar, and black pepper. Stir well with a fork. Salt to taste. Keeps covered in the fridge for two to three days.

Butternut Vinaigrette

4 tablespoons roasted butternut squash
4 tablespoons filtered water
2 tablespoons apple cider vinegar
1 ½ teaspoons maple syrup
½ teaspoon cayenne pepper
1 teaspoon sea salt
3 tablespoons olive oil

1. Combine the butternut squash (which can be roasted beforehand and kept in the fridge), water, apple cider vinegar, maple syrup, and spices in a blender or food processor.

2. Pulse while slowly adding olive oil to mixture. Taste and add more maple syrup or salt to taste.

Sherry Vinaigrette

2 teaspoons grain mustard
4 teaspoons sherry vinegar
3 tablespoons grapeseed oil
2 teaspoons water
1 teaspoon sea salt
½ teaspoon black pepper
½ shallot, finely minced

1. Combine the sherry vinegar and mustard and begin whisking. Slowly add 2 tablespoons of grapeseed oil while continuing to whisk.

2. Add the water and minced shallot, salt and pepper to taste, and give it a final mix.

Red Wine Vinaigrette

4 pickled grapes (pg. 79)
2 tablespoons red wine vinegar
2 tablespoons olive oil
2 tablespoons grapeseed oil
1 clove garlic, minced
1 teaspoon shallot, minced
salt and pepper to taste

1. Shake excess pickling juice from the pickled grapes and slice them in half, put four halves aside and combine the rest with vinegar, olive oil, and garlic in a blender.

2. Pulse the mixture while slowly drizzling the grapeseed oil. Season to taste.

3. Pour dressing into a small bowl and add minced shallot and a mince of the remaining pickled grapes.

Holy Daze Harissa

Makes 4 cups

Having no god and preferring few gifts, all we have is food when it comes to the holy days of winter. And so we tend to roar our oven with reckless abandon. But if there's one complaint we have with Thanksgiving and Christmas cooking, it's the general lack of hot sauce. Sloshing Sriracha, Tapatio, or Frank's Red Hot on top of a four-hour gravy seems sacrilege, and more than a little confusing. We finally solved our sauce dillema: Christmas harissa. We start with a base of our beer-braised cranberry sauce. Blended with a slew of roasted chiles, it comes out slightly sweet, very tart, and spruced with a subtle clove essence. One part sweet-inducing sting, one part chai-spice tongue comforter.

BEVERAGE

Fantôme Spéciale
De Nöel

SOUNDTRACK

Woods
"Twisted Tongue"

> 12 dried large red chiles (California or New Mexico)
> 6 fresh jalapeños
> 6 yellow wax peppers
> 2 poblano peppers
> 1 cup Krieked Cranberries (pg. 53)
> ½ cup cider vinegar
> ½ cup olive oil
> 1 tablespoon kosher salt
> 1 tablespoon clove
> sea salt to taste

1. Preheat the oven to 375 degrees while you deal with the chiles. Wearing gloves, slice open the dry chiles and place in a large bowl. Cover with a cup of warm water to rehydrate.

2. Slice the jalapeños, wax peppers, and po-blanos and remove the seeds. Place chiles in a bowl and spray with canola oil, dump onto a sheet pan and put into oven. Roast for about twenty to thirty minutes, until outer peppers start to blacken. Remove and let cool.

3. In a food processor, pulse the rehydrated red chiles, the roasted peppers, and cran-berry sauce. Slowly add vinegar and olive oil. Continue to blend for at least a minute to guarantee creamy consistency. If it appears goopy, add the leftover red chile water one tablespoon at a time. Add salt and spices and pulse some more.

4. Remove and store in the refrigerator. Harissa will keep for several weeks.

Celeriac Waldorf with Remoulade

Serves six

The Waldorf is one of those salads you can't quite believe exists until you encounter it face-to-face. We came face-to-faceplant while eating an "orphan's" Thanksgiving dinner during college with a roommate's family. Waiting for our Tofurkey to roast—so 2001, right?—we walked by the set dining room table and peeped some cute crystal bowls of chopped apples and nuts, peeled grapes, and celery slivers. "At least something's spared of Turkey and heavy cream," we thought... right before watching our buddy's grandma dispatch a scoop of Hellman's mayo all over each of the fruit bowls. Intent on conquering our crippling fear of this salad, we have come to reimagine the Waldorf in terms that we understand: tart fruits, soft winter vegetables, cracked nuts, and a handmade mayo. Winter's cole slaw is really what this is. But you can keep telling Grandma it's a Waldorf if it helps.

BEVERAGE

Kulmbacker
Eisbock

SOUNDTRACK

Belle and Sebastian
"The Model"

1 celeriac
2 medium-sized Fuji apples
½ cup walnuts (preferably in shell)
1 cup pickled grapes
a sprig of fresh dill for garnish
1 cup mayonnaise (pg. 62)
sea salt to taste

1. Set a large pot to boil with salted water while you prepare the celeriac. Remove the outer skin, slicing off all the brown, leaving you with just the inner white root. Slice the root vertically into eight or so thin sheets, lay the sheets down flat and then cut into thin matchsticks. Set aside until the water boils.

2. Slice the apple into thin matchsticks of roughly the same size. Set in a bowl of water with half a lemon, to keep from browning.

3. Shell walnuts and toast on high heat in a small pan. Set aside to cool and chop with knife into a rough dust.

4. Once water boils, prepare a bowl of ice water. Blanch the celeriac matchsticks by dropping them into the boiling water for thirty seconds; quickly remove them and place them in the ice bath for several minutes.

5. Strain apple and celeriac and pat dry. Combine both in a large mixing bowl. Add sliced grapes, mayonnaise, and dill. Toss well with tongs. Serve and top with nuts.

Blistered Brussels Sprouts

Serves two

Rainy, lazy Sundays may best be passed by putting Sonic Youth's *A Thousand Leaves* on the record player, scorching a salad, tossing it with booze, and sitting down to eat with a glass of farmstead sour beer—all while wearing sweatpants. For this fall salad, we take the poetic thousand leaves maxim and go literal, plucking all the leaves from Brussels sprout globes until your bowl looks like handfuls of miniature Bibb lettuce. Spiked with sherry-braised nuts and tart, ruby-red cranberries, everything about this salad is a precious little gem.

> 2 pounds Brussels sprouts (8–10 sprouts)
> ¼ cup raw pistachios
> ⅛ cup dried cranberries
> ½ cup sweet sherry
> ¼ cup sherry vinaigrette (pg. 48)
> sea salt and pepper to taste

1. Shred the Brussels sprouts into individual leaves: chop off the bottom (reserve for stock) and roughly roll the sprouts between your thumb and forefinger to release the leaves. Some may be more stubborn than others and you can either pry the leaves apart or cut an additional quarter inch off the base.

2. Braise the nuts and dried cranberries by adding them to a small saucepan, dousing with sherry and placing on medium heat, turning to a simmer as soon as you hit a boil. Simmer like this for fifteen minutes or until liquid is all but gone.

3. Heat a large skillet for a couple minutes on high heat, add the remaining 1 tablespoon of oil and make sure pan is well coated before tossing in the Brussels sprout leaves. Toss them in the pan every ten to twenty seconds, until some of the leaves have brown specks. When cooked thoroughly, douse the leaves in your vinaigrette. Toss one last time and plate salad. Garnish each with a spoonful of braised nuts and berries. Eat immediately.

BEVERAGE

New Belgium La Folie

SOUNDTRACK

Sonic Youth
"Sunday"

LIPIDS

Cooking without fat is like dry-humping your lover. Cooking vegetables properly requires fat, whether you're roasting, frying, whipping, mashing, or garnishing.

Olive oil: This is the only time we're militant about virginity—if its not extra virgin we disavow it like a Turkish father-in-law. One way to guarantee you're not spending your weed money on blended bullshit is to buy oils that have certified, protected appellations, generally from Europe—look for DOP, AOC, AOP, and DOC regulation seals (wiki that shit, dudes). Ensure that the oil actually is 100 percent olive, and not cut with any expeller pressed shit. In general we like it hard, slow, and green, usually from Spain, Italy, or Portugal.

Butter: Cow fat's something we used to boycott and now use in a limited way. When we do, we do it for a reason, so it has to be good stuff. We prefer butter from Vermont, and we like it when the fat content is eighty-three percent or higher. Beurremont is our fave, followed by Plugra, but the Irish foil-wrapped stuff ain't bad. You'll tell the difference when your pan's not spitting watery butter at you. Yes, higher fat may technically be more destructive to mind and body, but when you wield powerful ingredients, you use less.

Grapeseed oil: Sometimes the awesome olive oil you bought is not ideal for frying or making emulsions. Heating oil strips it of the flavor you paid for, and mixing it in dressings sometimes ends in confusing tastes. We swear by grapeseed oil for most fat tasks: it's got a high smoke point; its

flavor is neutral; and it's not a nasty commodity crop like canola (shorthand for Canadian oil, low acid) nor is it not manufactured in some bloody mob game by the good folks at Monsanto. It's also good for you, as far as liquid fat goes.

When substituting, know your lipids. Replacing butter with olive oil is a bad idea unless you want sugar cookies that taste like olives. This is when we call in the reserve goops, namely Earth Balance and Veganaise.

Krieked Cranberries

Makes 2 cups

Living far, far away from any cranberry bogs, we've never had the pleasure of picking the tart little fuckers from their low, pink shrubbery, or manhandling them off a farmer's stand. But we can't holiday-gorge without them. One way we keep it interesting is to make them fraternize with other produce—oranges and fresh ginger—as well as beer and something sweeter than your average sugar—Belgian candi sugar, which is most commonly used for beer brewing and confectionary purposes. We like Lindemans cherry lambic for beer. But you could also use a darker cherry ale for a maltier treat. The best part? You can pulse the leftovers for a sick gin fizz.

1 bag (12 ounces) cranberries
2 ½ cups Lindemans Kriek
1 cup Belgian candi sugar (brown sugar works)
1 cinnamon stick
zest of 1 orange
1 teaspoon fresh grated ginger
½ teaspoon salt

BEVERAGE

Lindemans Kriek

SOUNDTRACK

Primal Scream
"If They Move, Kill 'Em"

1. Place cranberries in a pot and cover with beer; stir in candi syrup. Add cinnamon stick, orange zest, ginger, and salt. Place on medium heat and let cook until mixture hits a rolling boil. Reduce to simmer and let cook another ten minutes.

2. Mixture should be gooey; cranberries should have burst. Taste and sweeten more if desired. Remove from heat and cool.

TIP If you find yourself with leftovers, here's a tip for getting drunk on them: blend a cup of krieked cranberries with four shots gin, a splash of lime juice, then spritz with champagne, and garnish with a lime wedge for the holiday's most fucked up gin and juice.

Faux Gras

Makes two 6 ounce jars

When PETA moved into our Echo Park neighborhood, we didn't pay much mind. But then we learned about "Fine Faux Gras Challenge," a PETA-hosted recipe competition that's giving $10,000 to the creator of the most "palatable" imitation duck liver. The contest rules seemed loosey goosey: everything just had to be "vegetarian." Now that was a contest we knew we could jam hard! Before we go further, let us just say we love cooking vegan—but we dislike most vegan food products. We love vegetables in their natural shape and fake meats from scratch. That's why we knew we wanted to whip together a faux foie gras dripping with the unctuous pleasures of butter fat. So what happened with our foolproof entry? Well, we made it, tasted it, and wrapped it in a bow, only to find out that when PETA says "vegetarian" they mean "vegan." Let's just say we found new meaning to the phrase "faux pas." Oh well, more for us.

3 parsnips
1 cup raw cashews
3 cups cream sherry
8 ounces unsalted butter
2 teaspoons ground white pepper
1 gram agar agar
3 teaspoons sea salt
1 teaspoon pink peppercorns

TIP Skinning already roasted parsnips is tedious, but we promise it's better. If you peel the little fuckers and then roast them, they won't retain the same unctuous, moist flavor. What we found works best is take a fork to each parsnip sliver and run the tines in a downward motion away from you to scratch the surface just hard enough to slough off the peel.

BEVERAGE

Russian River Temptation

SOUNDTRACK

Pictureplane "Cyclical Cyclical (Atlantis)"

1. Preheat your oven to 350 degrees and make a double boiler by placing a pot filled with water and topped with a metal bowl on medium heat. Add butter.

2. Prepare parsnips, slicing them in half lengthwise and placing them skin side down in a roasting dish. Add 4 tablespoons melted butter, 1 teaspoon salt, and ½ cup sherry. Seal the roasting dish with aluminum foil and roast for about twenty-five minutes.

3. Toast cashews in a skillet on medium heat. Toss often to ensure even cooking. When the nuts start to brown, add 3 tablespoons melted butter. When the butter starts to brown, turn off heat and set the pan aside to let nuts finish cooking; they will absorb most of the butter. Once they've cooled, pulse them in a food processor to pulverize.

4. Check parsnips: you want them fork tender at their thickest. If not there yet, return to the oven and keep roasting. Check them every ten minutes until "fall apart tender." Remove and cool.

5. Scrape off all the parsnip skins with a fork. Mix parsnip flesh with 4 tablespoons melted butter in a bowl. Mash and add white pepper and remaining 2 teaspoons salt. Using a blender or food processor, combine with cashew dust and ½ cup sherry. Blend until it

resembles a smooth, pliable batter. Salt to taste.

6. Make a sherry gelée: pulverize the agar agar by crushing or chopping it as finely as possible. Add it to a sauté pan with ¾ cup sherry at medium heat until sherry nears a boil; don't let it actually boil. Whisk until the agar agar dissolves and makes a gel. Return to a low simmer.

7. Clarify the remaining butter, skimming off the layer of scum in your double boiler, and gently spoon everything but the watery separation into a new bowl. (When using high-fat butter, there will be very little water.) Keep the melted butter warm.

8. Scoop your parsnip-cashew mash into two mason jars, leaving at least two inches of space at the top of each jar for your butter and gelée layers. Smooth the top of the puree into a flat landscape with a small spatula and wipe the insides of each jar clean with paper towels.

9. Pour half the clarified butter on top of each jar, and immediately place in the freezer. The butter will harden and create a flat surface for the gelée.

10. Finish the gelée by giving it a final whisking. Remove from the heat and let it cool

for one minute, then pour on top of butter, dividing evenly between your two jars. Place the jars in the fridge to finish, and let sit for at least thirty minutes.

11. To serve, bring the faux gras up to room temperature, and garnish with sea salt and pink peppercorns. Serve on crusty bread.

Baby Baked Potatoes

Serves four

Babies are always cuter than what they grow up to be—even when they're baked. Fat, hulking Russets with their dirty, flappy skins stretched open and stuffed with oozy sour cream and sweaty onions—no one wants to see that, let alone eat it, at a party. But there is something undeniably sensual about serving our miniature, one-bite version. Pick up creamers or German butterball potatoes for this recipe: rounder potatoes are better. Topped with a splash of cream or veganaise and a sprinkle of bacony crumbles and chives, this is a snack-attack waiting to happen.

    10-12 baby potatoes
    3 tablespoons crème fraiche (pg. 62)
    1 teaspoon ground black pepper
    1 teaspoon finishing salt
    2 tablespoons Magic Shroom Dust (pg. 30)
    1 sprig fresh dill
    1 small bunch chives, minced

1. Scrub all your potatoes under cold running water. Look at your potato like it's an egg. Slice the skin off of the lengthwise edges on the left and the right sides of your theoretical ovum. Need another analogy? Make two slices on either side of the potato so that the apex of the parenthesis is flat. Whatever.

2. Now, slice each potato in half right down the middle, to make the now completely exposed face the "top" and the sliced face that you just figured how to do the "bottom." Using a metal measuring spoon (teaspoon size preferred) or a melon baller, gently scoop out a half sphere in the center of each potato. Be careful to not dig too deep. Repeat until your baby potatoes become twice as many potato cups.

3. Now place all the potatoes in a large pot and cover with cold water. Salt the water liberally, and then turn the flame on high. When the water boils, your potatoes are done. Drain and sit in cool water for a few minutes.

4. Preheat oven to 350 degrees and grease a baking tray. Flicking potato cups dry place

them face down on tray and bake for ten to twelve minutes or until slightly brown. Remove, let cool, then plate.

5. Mix the crème fraiche with the black pepper. Using a spatula or a pastry bag, fill each potato cup with the peppery crème. Carefully garnish with dill tops, chives, salt, paprika, and Magic Shroom Dust.

BEVERAGE

Hair of the Dog Fred from the Wood

SOUNDTRACK

The Stooges
"Little Doll"

Savory Rolls

Serves eight

Nothing satiates the sentient like the gooey, almost raw central mass of a freshly baked sweet roll. As true seekers of new ways to sedate each other with homebaked carbs, we flipped the Cinnabon on its noggin' one New Year's Day and whipped up what has become our favorite recipe for savory rolls. Take everything sweet about a cinnamon roll and invert it: soft sweet bread becomes tart and savory, gooey brown-sugar butter morphs into salty caramelized shallot goo, and frosting slumps into melted aged cheese. Yeah this will take a few hours to a day... but it will hurt your friends and lovers in the most wonderful way.

SPONGE STARTER
(You will have leftovers)
2 ½ cups all-purpose flour
2 cups filtered water
¼ teaspoon dry active yeast

DOUGH
1 cup sponge (above)
1 large egg
1 teaspoon salt
1 teaspoon baking powder
1 teaspoon baking soda
1 teaspoon instant yeast
1 tablespoon brewer's yeast
2 cups all-purpose flour
¼ cup water
¼ cup melted butter (margarine works)
1 teaspoon olive oil

FILLING
1 cup Cast-Iron Mushrooms (pg. 29)
2 pounds shallots, sliced
½ cup cream sherry
2 cups chopped dill
½ pound shredded aged cheese (we use Comté)
sea salt and pepper

1. Combine all sponge starter ingredients in a mixing bowl. The resulting goo should look wet and reckless. Wrap the bowl up and let it sit in the corner (preferably a warm one) for four hours or as long as overnight.

2. Combine all the dry ingredients for the dough in a large bowl or the mixing bowl for a counter top mixer. Mix them, mechanically or manually, so that all they are distributed evenly. Add water, one cup of the sponge, and butter and mix to combine.

3. Add the egg. You want to do this after the butter so the egg doesn't cook. Mix by hand for ten to fifteen minutes (three to five with a Kitchen Aid using the paddle on medium speed) until the dough forms a smooth paste. It should still be sticky and stretchy, but not very wet. If you're using a machine; switch to the dough hook and mix for another five minutes on medium; if you're manual, turn the dough out on a floured surface and knead the hell out of it for seven minutes.

4. In yet another bowl, add the olive oil and give a swirl. Form the dough into a ball, and roll it in the oil so that it's greasy everywhere. Cover the bowl with plastic and let it sit for an hour in a warm corner.

5. For filling, make Cast-Iron Mushrooms but add 2 pounds of sliced shallots. When the shallots begin to brown, add ½ cup cream sherry and reduce by half. Set aside.

6. Form the rolls: on a floured surface, gently roll out the dough into a 12 by 18 inch square. Spread the sherry-butter-shallot-mushroom goo all over the giant dough square on your counter. Make sure to spread evenly all the way to the edges. Apply the dill and the cheese in a similar fashion; evenly distribute all the way to the corners of your dough sheet.

7. Sprinkle salt and grind pepper all over the thing and preheat your oven to 350.

BEVERAGE
Bear Valley Black Flag
Imperial Stout

SOUNDTRACK
Inca Ore
"The Birds in the Bushes"

Continued on next page ∵

HOT KNIVES | SALAD DAZE

•: Continued from previous page

8. As if it were a joint—that's right—carefully roll the rectangle into itself. Start at the bottom and curl inwards until you have a bulging log. Use a sharp knife and slice rolls off of the left side of the log. You can make them as thick as you'd like; we like ours about two inches thick.

9. Gingerly place the rolls side by each on a greased (with butter) baking pan and cover them loosely with plastic.

10. When thirty minutes—minimum!—has elapsed, slide the rolls into the oven and bake for fifteen to twenty minutes. When they start to smell amazing, check them. You're looking for a nice golden brown hue on the top of each one.

Ve **Melted Endive**
VEGAN

Serves four

Our friend Claire's mom has always intimidated us. Sharp, candid, and coolly dismissive, she's one of those moms that pulls off short hair, wears all black, and makes fun of you for not partying hard enough. It doesn't hurt that she's French. We were still in college when she came over for dinner once and chopped circles around us by whipping up a basic ratatouille of eggplant, onion, fennel, and endive and plopping it on the table like it was "pooofff—nothing—what?" Molten-soft and warming, this dish had our young hearts at first bite, but still it took us years before we had the balls to go after it. Now, we're a little older and wiser. We know it's really all about precise knife skills, maintaining a proper roasting dish, and the timing of your movements, and we'd gladly risk the tsk-tsking of Claire's mom to cook our streamlined version for her. A total MILF if there ever was one—mother we'd like to feed!

> 6 heads Belgian endive
> 1 large fennel bulb
> 1 red onion
> 3 tablespoons olive oil
> 1 tablespoon balsamic vinegar
> 1 tablespoon fresh thyme leaves
> sea salt and pepper to taste
> 2 ounces Comté (optional)

BEVERAGE

Verhaeghe Duchesse de Bourgogne

SOUNDTRACK

Françoise Hardy "Tous les garçons et les filles"

1. Prepare the endive by trimming the woody base and slicing each head in half; set aside. Trim the base and top of the fennel (reserve fronds for other use) and cut in half, and then slice each half into six or so quarter inch thin pieces. Peel and cut the red onion in half, then carefully slice into a dozen or more half-moons. Preheat oven to 350 degrees.

2. Dash about half your oil into a medium-sized roasting dish (rectangular is better than square for this) and rub with your fingers to distribute. Arrange the vegetables neatly by placing one endive half against the pan (with its open side pointing out and rounded side against the pan) followed by a fennel slice and an onion slice. Do this until you fill the pan with tightly packed slices of endive, fennel and onion. Top this with the remaining olive oil and slide into the oven.

3. Cook the vegetables for about twenty-five minutes. Once vegetables start to show a little color, remove the pan and drizzle balsamic vinegar on top. Return to the oven for another ten minutes. Finish by placing under the broiler for one to two minutes. Remove and let cool.

4. Serve warm with thyme, sea salt, freshly cracked pepper, and, if desired, a pinch of grated Comté.

GREEN GOD OIL

MULLED MAPLE SYRUP

Condiments

The best way to banish weird chemicals from your
pantry is to make sauces yourself.

CRÈME FRAICHE

WOOSTER SAUCE

CLASSIC MAYO

Mayonnaise

Makes 2 ½ cups

> 2 egg yolks
> ½ cup grapeseed oil
> ½ cup olive oil
> ½ lemon
> 1 tablespoon sherry vinaigrette (pg. 48)
> (or ½ a shallot sat in 1 tablespoon sherry
> vinegar)
> 1 teaspoon sea salt
> cracked black pepper

1. Crack eggs and separate yolk into a medium-sized mixing bowl. (Reserve whites for baking or discard.) Beat yolks well with a whisk to get started

2. Slowly drizzle half the grapeseed oil while steadily whisking. Next, drizzle half the olive oil. Repeat. Add lemon, peeled and minced shallot, salt, and pepper, and whisk until your arm hurts and mayo has a light yellow custard consistency. With really big-ass yolks, add more liquid.

Crème Fraiche

Makes 2 cups

> 2 cups heavy cream
> 3 tablespoons cultured buttermilk
> 1 teaspoon sea salt

1. Mix the two cow juices in a non-reactive, preferably non metallic container. Cover with plastic wrap, and let ferment at room temp, or a little warmer, for about twenty-four hours.

2. After a day, remove your wrap and check the cream. It should essentially hold its shape if you slosh the fermenting vessel. Small bubbles may have formed: this is totally cool.

3. Stir the mixture with a spatula or spoon and taste it: it should be tart, creamy (duh), but you'll find that it's surprisingly light for essentially being curdled whipping cream. Keeps in the fridge for weeks.

Green God Oil

Makes 1 cup

> 2 cups fennel fronds
> 1 bunch flat leaf parsley
> ½ bunch chives
> 2 tablespoons kosher salt
> 1 cup grapeseed oil

1. Bring a large pot of water to a boil, add salt, and prepare your greens for blanching. Trim the the top stem of a fennel bulb; you'll use only the wispy fronds not the stalks. Chop the stems off your parsley bunch. Prepare an ice bath by putting water and ice in a large metal bowl.

2. Drop all the greens in the boiling water and leave for fifteen seconds. Then quickly fish them out with a strainer and dump in ice bath and leave there for a minute.

3. Place a towel or paper towel on a large plate. Once greens are cool, remove, shake, and let sit on the plate to dry.

4. Roughly tear or chop the dry blanched greens and add to a blender with a quarter cup of grapeseed oil. Pulse and slowly drizzle another quarter cup and blend for thirty seconds, then add the remaining greens. Continue pulsing and drizzle in the rest of the oil, blending for another minute or so.

5. Pour this blended green mixture into a jar or other container with a top, sit in the fridge overnight or a day, to develop color.

6. Pour green mixture through a fine mesh strainer to remove any fibrous material. Use a spatula or ladle to help push the oil through. Keeps for several days covered in the fridge.

"Extra Olive" Olive Oil

Makes 1 cup

½ cup extra virgin olive oil
½ cup black dry-cured olives
(twenty olives)

1. Pit the cured olives and combine with half the olive oil in a food processor and pulse for several minutes, drizzling in the remainder slowly. Stop to scrape down the sides with a spatula as needed.

2. Let sit like this for one hour. Then pulse again.

3. Strain the olive chunks out and collect just the oil, which should be dark brown. Use in place of olive oil for heavy olive taste.

Wooster Sauce

Makes 1 ½ cups

1 ounce tamarind paste
4 tablespoons balsamic vinegar
4 tablespoons white distilled vinegar
4 tablespoons filtered water
1 tablespoon molasses
2 tablespoons soy sauce
1 tablespoon orange juice
¼ cup chopped white onion
1 teaspoon grapeseed oil
3 whole cloves
1 teaspoon nutritional yeast
1 teaspoon paprika

1. Blend tamarind paste, vinegars, molasses, water, soy sauce, and orange juice in a blender.

2. Cook it to gel flavors. In a sauce pot with oil, sauté onion for several minutes, until slightly translucent, and add the blended mixture plus cloves and orange zest. Heat on medium high until mixture boils, then remove and let sit to cool.

3. Return to blender. Add yeast, paprika, and any additional salt and pepper to taste, and pulse. Strain through a fine mesh strainer and store.

Mulled Maple Syrup

Makes 4 cups

4 cups maple syrup (B Grade)
2 cardamom pods (or 1 teaspoon ground)
4 star anise
6-8 cinnamon sticks
2 fresh vanilla bean pods scraped
2 teaspoons peppercorns
1 nutmeg, smashed
6 cloves
1 orange

1. Dump the syrup into a heavy-bottomed pot and add all spices. Save the bottle for later use.

2. Peel the orange, creating several large pieces of peel, and add it to the pot (save the fruit for eating).

3. Place pot on low heat for several hours, checking on it every thirty minutes to stir and keep from scorching.

4. When you remove from heat, let it cool completely, at least one hour, before returning to the bottle.

Warm Niçoise

Serves two

The times we've visited the South of France in winter, all we craved were hot stews, soft baguette, and a wool peacoat. Salad certainly didn't come to mind. But hearty vegetables that've been parboiled, gently fried, and fire roasted with herbs, olives, lavender, and warm seeds is a very different thing. These are flavors that feel and taste to us like warm soil—a blanket of soft earth keeping us warm in hibernation. No tuna—the sea's the last place you want to be. No egg—that'd mean coming to the surface. Just lying in a garden bed waiting for spring.

4 fingerling potatoes
2 cups green beans, trimmed
2 tablespoons "Extra Olive" Olive
   Oil (pg. 63)
1 tablespoon pumpkinseed oil
1 teaspoon champagne vinegar
1 teaspoon smoked paprika
Maldon salt to taste

TAPENADE DE PROVENCE
1 red bell pepper
¼ cup pepitas (raw)
1 teaspoon fresh thyme leaves
pinch of fresh lavender

1. Put whole fingerlings in a medium-sized pot of salted water and place on high heat. Once you hit a boil, remove the potatoes from the water but keep water boiling. Add green beans and let cook for one to two minutes, until bright green.

2. Prepare an ice bath. When green beans have cooked enough, strain and dunk them in ice water. Let sit.

3. Roast the red bell pepper directly on the stove, turning every couple minutes. Once charred, sit it in a bowl covered with a plate to loosen skin. Meanwhile, toast pepitas on high heat, tossing every thirty seconds to keep from burning. Once they start to brown, remove and let sit in the pan for five minutes.

4. Peel the pepper by sloughing off charred skin by hand and brushing dry; slice into four sections, remove seeds, and mince. In a bowl, combine the pepitas, minced pepper,

thyme leaves, lavender, and Maldon salt. Stir to mix and set aside.

5. Heat a skillet on medium heat. Slice each fingerling into four or five round pieces and toss with "extra olive" olive oil, then toss in the pan and cook for a minute or two on each side, just enough to get some color. Set pan aside but keep potatoes warm.

6. Dry roast the beans by shaking them dry and adding to a skillet with no oil. Stir or toss to cook evenly. You want them to pop slightly and blacken without burning. Remove and toss with pumpkinseed oil and champagne vinegar.

7. Plate by lining up a dozen or more dressed beans in the middle of a plate. Top with carefully arranged potatoes and the tapenade mixture, garnish with smoked paprika.

BEVERAGE
Telegraph Stock Porter

SOUNDTRACK
Air
"J'ai dormi sous l'eau"

Winter Lettuce Consommé

Serves two

Sometimes the prospect of making soup is beholden to one's sense of commitment. Not only is it a time-consuming task, but it presupposes success and duration: the soup rules the kitchen and it will be eaten in all its big-pot, cook-everything-in-your-fridge glory over two days by you and your lover/roomie/friends. This is not that kind of soup. This is a soup course for those times when you don't want to spend all day hovering over a pot; when a soothing, salty broth is what you yearn for; and when you need a quick and easy way to turn some of that lingering salt murk that has now taken over part of your fridge (i.e. kimchi brine), and create a simple but crazy good dish that can be made to scale within one hour. While this ain't yer mom's chicken noodle soup (duh, no noodles [and no chicken]), it just might cure what ails you.

> 1 cup kimchi brine (pg. 20)
> 2 stalks lemongrass
> 4 cups filtered water
> 1 small Napa cabbage
> 2 turnips
> 2 handfuls arugula
> ⅛ cup cilantro leaves, picked
> ⅛ cup flat leaf parsley leaves, picked
> 1 tablespoon Green God Oil (pg. 63)

1. Combine 1 cup of reserved kimchi brine and at least 4 cups of filtered water in a pot; taste and dilute more if too salty for you. Take the lemongrass stalks and beat them firmly against a wood cutting board several times, to soften. Cut each stalk into four or five pieces and add to the pot. Boil for twenty minutes.

2. Pick several outer Napa cabbage leaves and add to the boiling broth. Peel your turnips and trim the stem enough to sit the turnip flat on a cutting board then throw the skin and trims in the pot. Lower the broth to a simmer. Cook for at least thirty minutes, then remove all the solid cooked veggies and compost them.

3. Carefully slice the turnips as close to an eighth inch as you can, maintaining their shape. Gently place in the simmering pot. Let this simmer for about ten minutes.

3. Prepare a mixed green garnish of arugula and a few fresh, sliced Napa cabbage leaves, and place at the bottom of your soup bowls, alongside a mixture of whole parsley and cilantro leaves.

4. Once turnips are fully cooked, remove from heat. Gently scoop up half a turnip and place in each soup bowl atop your little salad. Bring the soup to a boil, and ladle the broth over the greens—essentially blanching them. Blow, slurp, swoon.

BEVERAGE

Stone, Victory, and Dogfish Head Saison du BUFF

SOUNDTRACK

Jesus and Mary Chain "Happy When It Rains"

Onion Soup Sandwich

Makes two

BEVERAGE

Rodenbach Classic Red

SOUNDTRACK

Serge Gainsbourg
"Aux armes et cætera"

Of the five trophies we've taken at the Grilled Cheese Invitational over the years, our favorite is this amalgamation sandwich that uses our beer-infused Belgian Onion Soup. The Trappist beer–laden onions mimic soup, while the crisp cheese-toast and oozy cheese emulate the gooey crouton on top. There's only one way to eat this sammich: we call it the "crunch-slurp" method.

1 cup Belgian Onion Soup (pg. 97)
2 tablespoons butter, room temperature
4 slices soft brioche
½ pound Gruyère cheese, grated
⅛ pound Parmesan, grated
1 tablespoon sharp grain mustard
2 sprigs fresh thyme for garnish
sea salt to taste

1. To reuse leftover soup for this recipe, strain any residual liquid, using only the onions.

2. Choose a pan (cast-iron!) wide enough to fit two sandwiches. Place pan on medium-high heat for up to five minutes, or until thoroughly hot. Turn down to medium and begin grilling.

3. Butter one side of each slice of bread. Top two of the slices with cheese and place them butter side down in the hot pan. It should sizzle but not too explosively. Using tongs, add about ½ cup serving of onion mixture to the cheese, followed by a knife's worth of grain mustard. Top both with the second slice of bread and press down carefully (use a pot or other heavy object for consistent weight).

4. Checking the bread that's face down every minute, let cook until bread is golden brown. Flip gingerly with a spatula, apply more butter and press down. Repeat until cheese is thoroughly melted.

5. Now create the Parmesan crust: remove both sandwiches and apply more butter to pan, then sprinkle Parmesan where each sandwich will sit. Quickly return both sandwiches and press. After a minute, repeat with other side.

6. Remove sandwiches from heat. Let sit for two minutes under a bowl, to let the cheese settle and gel, then slice and serve. Garnish with thyme leaves.

ACIDS

If you want to separate the gold from the shit, here's a tip: think about vinegar the way you do whiskey. Is it old? Is it blended? Is it aged in a barrel? Vinegar, our favorite (non-psychedelic) acid is loin-sweat of the gods; it needs a long nap in wood to really make our guts grumble.

Balsamic is as beautiful as cave-aged barley-wine when it's real. Unfortunately, most of what's on US shelves is a lie. Read the ingredients: if there's anything other than the words "grape" or "must," you're fingering an imposter. Real balsamic is the leftovers from wine-making reduced in copper vats and then aged in up to six different types of wooden barrels. Don't buy balsamic from Italy for more than $5 unless it's certified as "Aceto Balsamico Tradizionale." Here in the states, Sparrow Lane, in Napa, makes a good-quality clone.

Cider should be tart and puckery, but never sour. We like to sip it like kombucha. The best French versions will taste like acidified Normandy cider (i.e. real cider), and there are a number of American producers who utilize specific apple varietals to great effect (Clovis, Sparrow Lane, etc.). Lots of local apple vendors at farmers markets also make a cider vinegar: Our local hero is Ha's Apple Farm.

Red wine is an easy vinegar to get swindled on cuz most varieties look like watery maraschino syrup. People don't know they're worth the good stuff! Red vinegars should taste like something other than acetic acid. You should get hints of the booze and the barrel. We use Banyuls and probably consume more aged grape juice through it than drinking actual wine.

Sherry for the most part tastes like nothing. The secret password to open up the world of good sherry vinegar is "Solera," which refers to a pyramid-scheme blending technique that is essential to getting good wood. Like blended scotch or gueuze, good sherry vinegar is made by blending younger barrel-aged vintages with older ones. When a bottle says "Solera 30" it means there's a thirty-year-old inside partying with teens to make a more full-flavored, complex explosion.

Winter Seitan, Spiced Carrots

Makes one loaf

Around the holidays, we become seitanists, devotees of doughy slices of crispy blackened wheat gluten that stays juicy inside. We sift the flour with a mix of winter spices—crushed fennel seed, ground sage—and encrust it with whole pink peppercorns. Since the human desire to stuff foods with other foods is nearly irresistible around the holidays, you wouldn't be wrong to serve this seitan with a side of stuffing (pg. 89) but be prepared for a carb-on-carb encounter (kinda like a bread version of turducken). For that reason, try it lighter with spice-glazed carrots and a pillow of coconut mashed potatoes (pg. 73). Hail seitan.

WINTER SEITAN
3 cups gluten flour
1 cup whole wheat pastry flour
2 tablespoons fennel seed
1 tablespoon ground sage
1 tablespoon onion powder
1 tablespoon nutritional yeast
1 teaspoon cayenne pepper
2 teaspoons smoked paprika
2 teaspoons kosher salt
1 teaspoon fresh ground pepper
3 ½ cups veggie stock (pg. 30)
½ cup grapeseed oil
¼ cup soy sauce
¼ cup olive oil
1 teaspoon pink peppercorns
canola oil spray

1. Preheat the oven to 375 degrees and prepare your counter space by laying out all the necessary dry ingredients, a measuring cup (1 cup), two large mixing bowls, a towel, a bread pan, aluminum foil, wax paper, olive oil, and canola spray.

2. Now mix the dry ingredients in one bowl: the flour, the spices, and salt. Finally grind the fennel seed coarsely in a mortar and pestle or with a knife (a clean coffee grinder also works) and toss that in, too.

3. In the second bowl, measure out the wet ingredients: stock, grapeseed oil, soy sauce (reserve olive oil for later). Whisk well.

4. Slowly pour about half the wet ingredients into the dry bowl and mix roughly with your hands. Flick off goo bits and towel dry hands. Pour in the rest of the liquid slowly in batches to mix thoroughly, saving a tablespoon or so

just in case. (You want a gloopy bread batter that sticks together if you try to flip it in the bowl but can also be easily pulled apart.) Add the last bit unless it seems too wet.

5. Take enough wax paper to line your bread pan. Spray the sides of the pan with a touch of canola, then lay it down. Spray even more on the top side of the wax paper to keep seitan from sticking. Grind a decent teaspoon or so of fresh black pepper in the pan.

6. You're ready to dump/slide the seitan blob into your lined bread pan. Coat with a touch of olive oil on top, more black pepper and seal with aluminum foil.

7. Finally make a double boiler by filling a large roasting dish one-third full with water and place the bread pan inside this roasting dish. Put the whole thing in the oven and

Continued on next page ∴

BEVERAGE

Gouden Carolus Cuvée
Van De Keizer Blauw

SOUNDTRACK

Electric Hellfire Club
"Incubus (Lætherstrip
Remix)"

∵ Continued from previous page

bake for an hour and thirty minutes, rotating after forty-five minutes.

8. Once time expires, pull loaf out and uncover. Check for doneness by poking with a fork. You want it pliable and slightly browned, but remember it will continue to firm up as it cools. Stick it in for a few more minutes for color and remove. Carefully flip the loaf over to eject from pan, gently unpeel any sticking wax paper. Let sit for at least ten minutes, then slice and sear both sides in a pan before serving.

SPICED CARROTS

2 dozen heirloom carrots
1 teaspoon olive oil
1 tablespoon butter
  (olive oil works)
1 tablespoon vadouvan (pg. 45)
2 tablespoons honey
  (agave works)
2 teaspoons water
sea salt to taste

1. Peel the carrots just enough to remove two-thirds of the skin but without stripping carrots of their color. Roughly chop the vadouvan.

2. Heat a large skillet on high heat, and add butter and oil. Let the pan get hot, then add carrots. Roughly chop or tear the vadouvan into pieces and add to the pan. Cook for several minutes while shaking every so often.

3. In a small bowl, whisk honey with a touch of water to thin, set aside.

4. Once carrots are slightly undercooked, add honey mixture and toss to cover; let cook another two to three minutes to reduce the glaze. Salt to taste and serve.

Coconut Mashed Potatoes

Serves four

Dismissing mashed potatoes as a thoughtless side dish—or one to be assigned to the worst cook among your family members—should be a crime punishable by a whack with the potato masher. Sure, as Americans we feel like potatoes are just waiting to bend to our will and become creamed, fried, or krinkle-cut to perfection. But fresh potatoes are serious tubers that require skill and planning. The perfect mash requires three things: enough fatty oils for taste, warmed liquid for aeration, and an exact cooking time to fully soften the starches without over-cooking them. Perfect vegan mashed potatoes require extra care and cost—we like the hippy-dippy gut bomb that is pure coconut oil—and doling out tough love to your gently cooked potatoes, by beating the pure shit out of them.

> 4 large russet potatoes
> 4 cloves garlic, peeled and minced
> ⅓ cup coconut oil
> ⅓ cup margarine
> 1 cup coconut milk
> 1 tablespoon onion powder
> 1 tablespoon sea salt
> 1 tablespoon fresh ground pepper
> Holy Daze Harissa for garnish (pg. 49)

1. Peel your potatoes, removing skin completely. Chop into large consistent cubes about an inch wide and place submerged in a large pot of cold salted water. Bring this pot to a boil on high heat.

2. Let the potatoes hit a steady boil and continue cooking about two to three minutes, then remove from heat. A knife should slide evenly through a potato cube. Dump pot into a strainer to drain, return cooked potatoes to your large pot.

3. Take the smallest saucepan you have and place it on low heat. Add margarine and half the garlic. Sauté for a few minutes, making sure not to burn or even brown the garlic; remove from heat and let sit until ready to use.

4. Mash the potatoes by adding coconut oil and garlic-margarine, followed by onion powder and raw garlic. Beat well for several minutes before adding half the coconut milk; keep mashing. Add the rest and mash until completely smooth. Season with salt and pepper. Keep them on a simmer until ready to serve.

BEVERAGE

Maui
CoCoNut Porter

SOUNDTRACK

The Clash
"Safe European Home"

Fennel Kraut

Makes one week's worth

One October a couple years ago, we staged what we lovingly referred to as "Krautfest" on the patio of Verdugo Bar, one of our favorite LA beer joints. While Neu! and Can ejaculated from the speakers, several dozen muscle-bound beer-geek boys and girls lined up to pommel one another in a serious arm wrestling contest. Meanwhile, we were at the grill selling faux sausages boiled in black beer and grill grease, slipped into tiny buns and slathered with sharp mustard. To finish things off, each brat got a massive pile of either "borscht blast" or "garden green" homemade sauerkraut that had been stinking up our kitchens for weeks. Out of that Germa-phile festival was born our deep love of sauerkraut. Even though we made many batches of kraut, there was only one that made us stop and goosestep for joy: Fennel Kraut. The triumvirate of fermented fennel bulb, fresh fennel fronds, and fennel seed is powerfully unified. Like licking licorice goo off a boot.

1 small fennel bulb with fronds
1 green cabbage
½ white onion
4 tablespoons kosher salt
2 tablespoons black peppercorns
2 tablespoons white wine vinegar
   (distilled white vinegar works)
1 teaspoon fennel seeds

Beverage
Lindemans Gueuze
Cuvée René

Soundtrack
Neu!
"Neuschnee"

1. Use a mandolin and a large mixing bowl to slice the fennel and cabbage for saltings; start by cutting the fennel bulb in half, removing the stalks. Quarter the cabbage and remove (and discard) the core. Now, slice both on the mandolin in two batches. Do half the fennel and half the cabbage. Slice a quarter of the onion on the mando. Sprinkle half the salt on all of the above. Scrunch mixture for at least a minute, until fully mixed and depleted in size. This will make the cabbage release its own juice and mix with salt to form a brine. Toss in peppercorns. Transfer the mixture to a ceramic container for fermenting.

2. Repeat with the second half of the cabbage, fennel, onion, and spices.

3. Press the mix down hard, making sure its covered with the brine liquid. Place the kraut vessel somewhere in your kitchen where it's out of the way and at constant room temperature. Age for one to two weeks, tasting every day. Don't be afraid of any scum that forms on top of the brine; scoop it off and discard. As long as the veggies stay totally submerged, there's no way they'll spoil.

4. When the kraut reaches a funk level you like, finish by tossing with splash of vinegar and the fennel seeds. Serve with a nice garnish of chopped fennel fronds. We serve with mustard and seared figs.

All Tomorrow's Dumplings

Serves eight

Wilted salads. Congealed sauces. Cold, rock-hard, frost-bitten vegetables. There's little to like about leftovers. (Just consider the two words separately: Left. Over. Sad...) So we knew we'd stumbled upon the best thing since lemons-to-lemonade, cocaine-to-crack, when we realized that the fatty fluff of coconut mashed potatoes makes the perfect potato dumpling. Kneaded into a dough, cut into cute wafers, boiled, and pan-fried, these suckers are like gnocchi and Gushers candy rolled into one. Try 'em with any sauce. We are partial to cloaking them in harissa cream, Sage Pesto (pg. 37), or Butternut Vinaigrette (pg. 48).

2 cups leftover mashed potatoes
2 cups all purpose flour
½ cup hot water
extra flour for dusting
2 tablespoons olive oil
sea salt to taste
sauce of your choice

1. Combine the leftover mash with all-purpose flour in a bowl, dust your hands with flour, and mix. Slowly add hot water and continue mixing the flour and mash with your hands until you form a supple dough. Add until dough is no longer sticky.

2. Now, form the dumplings: dust a cutting board with extra flour and place the dough on it. Knead gently but firmly for a few minutes to distribute evenly. Using a rolling pin, gently roll out the dough into a ½-inch thick sheet. Using a 1-inch wide bottle cap, portion off quarter-sized morsels, and place on a flour-dusted surface. As you do this, bring a large pot of salted water to a hearty boil.

3. Drop the dumplings in the boiling water in batches of six to eight; wait about one minute, or until they completely float to the surface, and spoon them out with a strainer. Set aside to rest on a greased sheet while you finish boiling the whole batch.

4. To sauté: heat a large non-stick pan on medium heat, add olive oil, and toss in a handful of dumplings; cook for a few minutes, tossing often to keep from sticking. Once the outside has browned, remove and cloak in your sauce of choice.

TIP We find the classic gnocchi shape mildly annoying because it requires finnicky rolling and fork-pressing. To streamline, we use a plastic bottle cap from any old condiment in the pantry. Our fave is the neon-green top to our rice vinegar. It's an inch wide and slightly less deep with a round indentation at the very inner top. Using this as your cutter, merely press down quick and hard on the dough and then tap the bottle cap into the palm of your other hand to loosen the shaped dumpling.

BEVERAGE
AleSmith Decadence

SOUNDTRACK
Nirvana
"Sliver"

Chestnut Crepes, Persimmon Jam

Serves six

Persimmons—so cute, yet so cum-smelling. We sought a sweet, spiced way of eating these orange orbs to justify sitting them on our table around Thanksgiving. The answer: swim them in a candy-spice syrup that's something like the post-meal breath mints that you find on the way out of Indian restaurants. This runny orange jam is great on toast, rolls, ice cream, but it's a hands-down winner scooped inside a crepe. Don't stop there: cutting the all-purpose flour with chestnut flour gives it a brown, buttery winter edge; and adding curry to the batter brings the spicing full circle. No cum here.

PERSIMMON JAM
4 fuyu persimmons
1 lemon
1 ¼ cup brown sugar
1 cup warm water
6 whole cloves
1 teaspoon ground cardamom
1 tablespoon whole fennel seeds
1 teaspoon cider vinegar
a pinch of sea salt

CHESTNUT CREPES
¾ cup all-purpose flour
¼ cup chestnut flour
¼ cup crème fraiche (pg. 62)
¾ cup water
1 tablespoon curry powder
½ teaspoon kosher salt
canola spray

1. Prepare the persimmons: over a large mixing bowl filled with a cup of water and a squeeze of lemon, peel the skin away with a paring knife. As you finish peeling one fruit, place it in the bowl so it stays perky. Once all three are done, place them on a cutting board and slice them; cut into thin half-moons for a chunkier jam or dice them fine, whichever you prefer.

2. In a small sauce pot, combine warm water, sugar, and a teaspoon of lemon juice and stir to dissolve sugar. Add persimmon slices and place on medium-high heat. Once mixture reaches a boil, add remaining spices and vinegar, stir, and lower to a simmer. Cook this way for twenty minutes or until syrup has thickened and reduced about an inch. Cool and reserve.

3. Measure out flours and combine in a large mixing bowl. Add curry powder and salt and stir. Measure out ¼ cup crème fraiche in the bottom of a measuring cup, and fill to the one-cup mark with filtered water. Stir well to combine. (You can replace crème fraiche

with heavy cream.) Marry the flour and crème-water in the mixing bowl.

4. Using a whisk, mix the dry and wet ingredients until you have a thin batter, much looser than pancake batter. Once there are no lumps, stop whisking and set aside.

5. Make the crepes heating a ten-inch non-stick pan on high heat. Spray enough oil to glaze the pan, and once it's nearly smoking add crepe batter with a ladle and quickly distribute evenly by grabbing the pan and making a circular motion. Let cook on the first side until some browning has occurred (one to two minutes), then gently slide the crepe off the pan and onto a plate. Return the pan to the flame, spray more oil and flip the crepe off the plate into the pan on its uncooked side. Let cook for twenty seconds and remove.

6. Serve the crepes as they are finished, laying them flat and spooning persimmon syrup in a thin row down the middle and then rolling them up tightly. Top with extra crème fraiche.

BEVERAGE
Lagunitas
Brown Shugga'

SOUNDTRACK
Tsegué-Maryam
Guèbrou
"Mother's Love"

Smashed Sunchokes

Serves four

Talk about confused. Not only does the "Jerusalem Artichoke"—better known as the sunchoke—have absolutely nothing to do with artichokes, but it's got no relation to that contested home to various peoples of The Book. It's actually an American OG tuber that has laid down roots everywhere from Nova Scotia to Georgia. That's fitting for this sunflower relative, because sometimes its downright confusing knowing what to do with it. Though often treated like a potato, it's got much less starch and more moisture, so it needs tweaked preparations. Whenever we start seeing these guys at the market we go nuts, which often results in gross overbuying. This recipe is a great way to immediately deal with your self-control problems. Think of it as sunchokes on sunchokes, the perfect remedy to its identity problems.

1 pound of sunchokes
½ cup of sherry, divided
2 tablespoons olive oil, divided
4 shallots, sliced
1 cup water
1 lemon

2 tablespoons crème fraiche
  (pg. 62)
2 teaspoons sea salt
10 chive batons, minced
2 teaspoons black pepper ground
1 teaspoon white truffle oil
  (optional)

Beverage

Bell's Kalamazoo Stout

Soundtrack

Swans
"I Am the Sun"

1. Scrub the sunchokes with cold water and pat dry; preheat your oven to 350 degrees.

2. Slice two-thirds of the sunchokes in half and toss them in a roasting dish with ½ cup of sherry, all the shallots, 1 teaspoon salt and 1 tablespoon olive oil. Seal the deal up with aluminium foil and bake for thirty minutes.

3. Slice the remaining third of your sunchoke stash in half, then cut each half in four by making two forty-five–degree cuts in each—the end result should be wedgelike in appearance. Squeeze the lemon into a mixing bowl with the water and add these pretty slices to the drink.

4. Check the guys in the oven. You're looking for fork-tender doneness.

5. Heat a medium-sized sauté pan on high heat. Sear the wedged sunchokes face down without oil for two minutes on each cut side. You want color. Add the olive oil, and the remaining sherry and cover. Cook on high for ten minutes and those guys will be done.

6. Remove the other sunchokes from the oven. Combine with the crème fraiche and pulverize by any means necessary. We use a large morter and a huge wooden club. Taste the mash and add all that pepper. Garnish with chives, truffle oil, and the stove-top braised sections of their brothers.

Pickles

Transform your farmers market spoils into forever babies.

OKRA

SUNCHOKES

APPLES

GRAPES

Apples

2 medium apples
1 cup filtered water
1 cup apple cider vinegar
2 tablespoons white sugar
1 tablespoon kosher salt
4 cloves
1 jalapeño
1 cinnamon stick

1. Wash and pat dry apples. Slice each apple lengthwise into six to eight round slices, flicking the seeds out of the middle. Arrange the slices in a clean, quart-sized jar with a rubber ring.

2. Prepare the pickling liquid. Set a pot of water to boil. In a large measuring device, measure out apple cider vinegar.

3. Slice the jalapeño lengthwise, from the stem to the tip, into four long slivers and break the cinnamon stick in half. Place the jalapeño, cloves, and cinnamon pieces into the jar.

4. Once water hits a rolling boil, add the apple cider vinegar, salt, and sugar and stir to dissolve, then quickly pour over the apples. The liquid should cover them. Place a saucer or rammekin on top of the apples to limit their contact with the air. Place in the fridge for at least one day and use within three to four weeks.

Okra

1 ½ pounds okra
1 quart plus 1 ½ cups filtered water
3 teaspoon kosher salt
3-4 dried chiles
4 sprigs fennel fronds
4 cloves garlic
4 cups distilled white vinegar
2 teaspoons sugar
1 teaspoon black peppercorns

1. Start with a brine: fill a large bowl with 1 quart water and 1 teaspoon kosher salt; stir to dissolve. Trim the woody stems from the okra and then add it the water; let sit covered for two hours.

2. After two hours, drain and rinse the okra pods and pat 'em dry with a clean towel. Stuff them creatively into the clean jar(s) and add garlic cloves, fennel fronds, and chiles.

3. In a stockpot, combine vinegar, 1 ½ cups water, sugar, peppercorns, and remaining 2 teaspoons of salt and bring to a boil on high heat. Let bubble for four minutes before turning off and using.

4. Pour the hot brine over the okra. Place a saucer or rammekin on top of the okra to limit their contact with the air. Age in the fridge for at least a day and use within three to four weeks.

Grapes

2 cups red grapes (about a pound)
1 cup filtered water
1 cup red wine vinegar
3 tablespoons white sugar
1 tablespoon kosher salt
1 teaspoon black peppercorns
1 teaspoon pink peppercorns

1. Wash and pat dry grapes. Arrange them in a clean, quart-sized jar with a rubber ring.

2. Prepare the pickling liquid. Set a pot of water to boil. In a large measuring device, measure out red wine vinegar.

3. Place the peppercorns in the jar.

4. Once water hits a rolling boil, add the vinegar, salt, and sugar and stir to dissolve, then quickly pour over the grapes. The liquid should cover them. Place a saucer or rammekin on top of the grapes to limit their contact with the air. Place in the fridge for at least a day and use within three or four weeks.

Sunchokes

1 pound sunchokes, roughly peeled
1 ½ cups apple cider vinegar
1 cup filtered water
2 tablespoons white sugar
2 tablespoons kosher salt
1 teaspoon black peppercorns
1 teaspoon turmeric powder
1 teaspoon coriander seeds
1 teaspoon fennel seeds
2 slices lemon

1. Start with a brine: fill a large bowl with 1 quart water and 1 teaspoon kosher salt, stir to dissolve. Add peeled sunchokes (some skin's okay) and let sit covered for two hours.

2. After two hours, drain and rinse the sunchockes, pat 'em dry with a clean towel. Stuff them into the clean jar(s) and add lemon slices and seeds.

3. In a stockpot, combine vinegar, 1 ½ cups water, sugar, turmeric, peppercorns, and remaining salt and bring to a boil on high heat. Let bubble for four minutes before turning off and using.

4. Pour the hot brine over the sunchokes. Place a saucer or rammekin on top of the sunchokes to limit their contact with the air. Age in the fridge for at least one day and use within three or four weeks.

Kohlrabi Latkes

Serves two

To the best of our knowledge, no processed food purveyor has created smoked salmon lox out of textured vegetable protein or pink-dyed soy—yet. This doesn't really bother us: we don't see the need to make squishy faux fish. Why try to fake it when nature's already handed you her best attempt? Roasted beets—especially golden or candy-striped ones—chilled and sliced paper-thin masquerades like some fucked-up imitation yellowfin, complete with marbled lines that look like shimmering fat deposits. Soaked in a vinegar and smoked salt bath, they're the closest you'll get to eating lox without catching monster fish as they spawn in the shadows of Mount Hood. We slide these suckers onto flash-fried latkes that've been perked up with apple—combinations that are real and deep and true. But what really sealed the deal for us was figuring out that a kohlrabi puree can replace the egg, and that extra shredded kohlrabi turns the world upside down.

BEET CARPACCIO
2 candy-stripe beets
1 tablespoon olive oil
1 teaspoon apple cider vinegar
1 teaspoon water
½ teaspoon smoked salt

KOHLRABI LATKES
2 kohlrabi
1 cup plus 2 tablespoons
    grapeseed oil
1 large russet potato
¼ cup chopped parsley
2 tablespoons crème fraiche
    (pg. 62)
1 teaspoon minced chives
2 slices pickled apples (pg. 79)
sea salt and fresh black pepper

1. Begin by roasting the two beets. Preheat the oven to 350 degrees; trim the beets' tips and base and wrap them in aluminum foil. Once the oven's hot, place the foil package inside and cook for about thirty-five minutes. Once steamy and fork tender, remove foil, and let beets cool for twenty minutes.

2. Peel beets by hand, or, using the aluminum to keep hands clean, rub the skins off and brush free of any clinging peel. Using a mandolin, slice the beets into a large mixing bowl and dress and toss with oil, vinegar, salt, and water. Place in a sealed container and refrigerate at least an hour, or up to several days.

3. Take the apple slices and dash with a touch of honey. Set aside.

4. Prepare a kohlrabi puree. Peel and chop one of the kohlrabi and place in a small sauce pot filled with water on high heat. Bring to a rolling boil and cook for five to eight minutes or until fork tender. Remove the kohlrabi pieces, pat dry, and pulse in a food processor while adding the two tablespoons of grapeseed oil until it forms an evenly whipped puree.

5. Peel and grate the remaining raw kohlrabi and potato on a box grater. Use immediately by combining in a large mixing bowl with the kohlrabi puree and chopped parsley; mix well by hand.

6. Fill a large heavy-bottomed pan with one cup of oil and place on high heat for several minutes. Once hot, form a couple latkes by cupping together with your hands and patting gently to form a half-inch cake. Fry a couple at a time, letting them cook undisturbed for two to three minutes or until you see the potato shreds browning nicely. Season liberally with salt and freshly cracked black pepper. Flip gingerly. After cooking another two minutes flip once more to ensure they've cooked evenly without burning. Remove and let cool on a paper towel. Repeat until all your latkes are done.

7. Plate the kohlrabi latkes and top with a dollop of crème fraiche, one or two slices of beet carpaccio, and pickled apple. Garnish with minced chives.

TIP For an even homier version, puree the pickled apples into a sweet-and-sour apple sauce. Add a handful of pickled apple slices to your food processor, add a touch of honey and a teaspoon of cinnamon. Use a bit of pickle brine to juice up the mixture.

BEVERAGE
Schmaltz He'Brew Bittersweet Lenny's R.I.P.A.

SOUNDTRACK
Built to Spill
"Distopian Dream Girl"

Golden Tagine

Serves four to six

Filed under "everything and the kitchen sink," tagine stew can be anything that's slow simmered in a pungent broth until it's soft. As much as we love the willy-nilly Berber-peasant concept of just naming this stew after the dish it's cooked in, we're too picky to allow our tagines to be catchalls for just any veggie. Instead, we use two anal-retentive organizing principles: taste and color. Slow stewing is perfect for a squash like kabocha because it turns hard and starchy in the oven but will then soak up a rich broth. For color, we turn to the turmeric yellow of golden beets, the bright orange of the squash, the army green of the okra; and the purple dye tone of Peruvian potatoes. Sounds like a tie-dye stew, come to think of it.

> ½ kabocha squash
> 2 golden beets
> 1 yellow onion
> 2 purple potatoes
> 1 ½ tablespoons olive oil
> 2 chipotle peppers in sauce
> 5 cups veggie stock (pg. 30)
> 1 teaspoon cardamom
> 1 teaspoon cumin
> 1 tablespoon sea salt
> 2 cinnamon sticks
> 10-12 spears pickled okra (pg. 79)
> parsley and mint sprigs
> Holy Daze Harissa (pg. 49)
> canola spray

1. Tackle the kabocha first. Preheat the oven to 325 degrees and use a long chef's knife to trim off the tips. Slice in half, and half again. Then cut the quarters into four or five half-moon slices, the shape you would for cantaloupe. Place flesh-side down on a greased cookie sheet and stick in the oven for about twenty minutes.

2. Prepare the other veg: peel and roughly chop the onion, slice the potato into six to eight large chunks. Peel the golden beets of their outer skin and stand them on their fattest end, slicing down the middle, spin and cut again into quarters, and repeat so you have 8 long slivers. Heat a large pot on medium heat, add olive oil, and toss in chopped onion. As soon as that starts to brown, add beet slices. Cook for five or so minutes, stirring frequently to prevent sticking. Now add the potato and set on medium heat.

3. Prepare your broth by combining veggie stock, chipotle pepper, hand-ground spices, and salt, and pulse in a blender. Dump this mixture into the pot, stir to distribute and let cook.

4. As soon as the kabocha squash is fork tender, but not yet browned, remove from oven and let cool. Once the pot nears a boil, set to simmer and add squash pieces and pickled okra. Stir and keep covered for ten to twenty minutes before removing from heat and serving.

5. To garnish, fish out cinnamon sticks and plug with fresh mint and parsley; deposit stuffed sticks on top of each bowl and surround with harissa.

BEVERAGE

Wetvleteren 12

SOUNDTRACK

The Cure
"If Only Tonight We
Could Sleep"

Sweet Potato Salad

Serves four to six

We always prefer fries to pies. And one of the sickest menu twists we ever saw to the now ubiquitous sweet potato–fries craze of 2010 was to serve them with creamy, well-salted blue cheese dressing. Aping that demented combination, we bring you the potato salad version. The clean crunch of celery and the tart sting of pickled apples manages to cut through the funky cream and gummy-sweet clouds of yams and potatoes. Of course, we panfried them, obliterating many of the health benefits.

2 sweet potatoes
2 yams
4 stalks celery, diced
4 slices pickled apple, diced (pg. 79)
¼ cup chives, minced
1 shallot minced
½ cup Blue Cheese Vinaigrette (pg. 48)
3 tablespoons mayonnaise (pg. 62)
½ cup cornmeal
1 tablespoon butter
sea salt and pepper to taste

1. Peel the yams and sweet potatoes, cut into one-inch cubes, and add to a large pot. Cover with salted water and place on high heat until you reach a boil.

2. As soon as the potatoes hit a boil, remove from heat and let sit for an extra two to three minutes. Make an ice bath in a large bowl. Drain the potatoes of the hot water and add them to the ice bath, letting chill for two minutes. Drain them of ice water and let dry.

3. Once potatoes are no longer wet, add to a large mixing bowl and toss with the cornmeal until each are covered. Heat a cast-iron on medium-high heat and add butter. Once butter is bubbling, add cornmeal-dusted potatoes. Fry for several minutes, stirring gently.

4. While still hot, combine pan-fried potatoes, blue cheese dressing, mayo, celery, apple, chives, and shallot. Mix with a spatula and season to taste.

BEVERAGE
Allagash Fluxus

SOUNDTRACK
Fela Kuti
"Gentlemen"

Apple Soup

Serves four

Some soups you want to sip, some you want to chug—and some, like this one, are so blissfully comforting you just want to fall asleep and die in them. A sort of fall lullaby, our apple soup is comprised simply of celery and apples two ways: a roasted apple-sauce stock and a chop of pickled apples. There's only one bit of foolery we introduce here: a chopped green tomato that masquerades as a green apple thanks to its color and tartness. Around late September, we start to see bushels and bushels of Fujis, Red Delicious, and Arkansas Blacks appearing at market, which is right around the time most of the country starts to see summer's tomatoes petering out, which means a ton of green tomatoes picked right before frost hits. The sweet-tart vibe is part of what makes this such a pleasure.

    4 large Fuji apples
    1 teaspoon caraway seeds
    1 teaspoon coriander
    2 tablespoons grapeseed oil
    1 tablespoon olive oil
    1 celeriac bulb
    2 celery stalks
    1 shallot
    1 large green tomato
    6 cups vegetable stock
    6-8 pickled apple slices (pg. 79)
    sea salt to taste

1. Start by making roasted apple sauce. Preheat oven to 300 degrees. Core and slice your apples in half or simply flick the seeds out. Grease a baking sheet with half the grapeseed oil and lay apples facedown; roast in the oven for about twenty minutes or until deflated and starting to brown. Remove and let cool until they can be handled. Toast the caraway and coriander seeds and add them with the apple mush to a food processor; pulse for thirty seconds or until pureed evenly.

2. Chop the vegetables: cut and clean your celeriac by removing the skin in down and outward cuts, chop the celery, and slice the shallots. Heat a soup pot on high heat, add the remaining grapeseed and olive oil, and toss in the cut vegetables.

3. Sauté for five to eight minutes, stirring often, until the shallots start to caramelize and the celeriac browns slightly. Then add the stock and reduce to a low heat, bringing to a slow boil.

4. Dice the green tomato into neat cubes the same size as the celeriac. Do the same with the pickled apple. Once the soup nears a boil, add both these. Once it starts boiling, cover and reduce to simmer for ten more minutes, then turn it off but keep it covered. Serve with minced chives or caramelized onions.

BEVERAGE

Port Santa's
Little Helper

SOUNDTRACK

Devendra Banhart
"Fall"

Grapevine Dolmas

Makes twenty

Stuffing grape leaves with pickled and dehydrated grapes falls under a broad category that we like to call Babies Dipped in Semen. Here's the idea: you take something and dip/wrap/stuff or otherwise manipulate it with a byproduct of itself. We think the origins were a spirited early morning conversation we had once about the culinary wonders of dipping a slice of tomato in ketchup. Ever since, we've been hooked on those dishes that avail themselves to BDS treatment. We've even found ourselves screaming the phrase in a bullhorn while selling food out of a food truck, to announce to a crowd of customers that they could now order an off menu treat comprised of truffle chèvre with fresh truffles grilled in truffle butter and then sprinkled with truffled salt. Babies dipped in sperm special! Admittedly, this is not an easy concept to sell to people while they're eating. But it *is* delicious.

> 20 grape leaves, packed in brine
> 1 cup jasmine rice
> 1 lemon
> 20 pickled grapes
> 1 cup golden raisins
> ¾ cup sunflower seeds, raw
> 1 ½ tablespoons za'atar
> ½ cup olive oil
> sea salt to taste

1. Cook the rice with 1 ¾ cups water and several slices of lemon in a pot over medium heat. Turn down after it hits a boil and let simmer for ten minutes, being sure not to overcook. Set aside.

2. Toast the sunflower seeds in a pan, adding za'atar about halfway through. As soon as seeds start to show color, remove from heat. Combine rice and spiced sunflower seeds in a large mixing bowl and toss with about one tablespoon olive oil, raisins, and salt to taste.

3. Rinse and pat dry your grape leaves to remove brine. Set up a rolling station with the leaves, a large plate, a shallow bowl with olive oil and a grill brush, and the bowl of rice. Remove twenty pickled grapes and start slicing them in half on a cutting board and set aside.

4. Assemble dolmas: lay one grape leaf down on the cutting board and lightly brush with olive oil. Then place a tablespoon or less of rice filling in the center of the leaf, forming it in the shape of a small log running horizontal to the leaf. Add two pickled grape halves on top of the rice log. Fold the left and right side in first and pinch while rolling the bottom away from you like a small burrito.

5. Collect the dolmas on a plate or in Tupperware and brush the outsides with extra olive oil.

BEVERAGE

Craftsman
Cabernale

SOUNDTRACK

The Muslims
"Walking With Jesus"

Pumpkin Ale Muffins

Makes six

We have zero reservations about drinking beer for breakfast. Why should we? Taken before noon it's more like medicine. Still, if you're not as liberal as we are with your a.m. libations, there is a way to consume without feeling like a scumbag: just replace the milk or water in your favorite muffin or pancake recipe with beer and you'll be eating your alcohol! Yeasty, wheaty, and a little effervescent, beer can actually make great baked goods even better. There's also something undeniably sick and satisfying about blending a beer smoothie at sunrise and pouring it into a batter. Now, the only question you should be asking is "which beer?" Listen up, because this may be the only time we'll ever utter these two words in the same breath: pumpkin beer. We usually mutter curses under our breath when we pass piles of this October trick in the shopping aisles. But bright orange and warmed with baking spices, we will never begrudge a pumpkin beer muffin.

½ sugar pumpkin
12 ounces pumpkin beer
1 ½ cups all-purpose flour
1 egg
1 stick butter, melted
1 ½ teaspoons baking powder
½ cup white sugar
3 tablespoons maple syrup
1 teaspoon ground cardamom
1 teaspoon nutmeg
1 teaspoon salt
zest of one orange

1. Preheat the oven to 325 then start in on the pumpkin. Chop off its top a few inches from the stem (reserve), and then cut the rest of it in half. Remove seeds. Now, place the pumpkin on a greased casserole dish and slide into the oven.

2. Let pumpkin roast for fifteen to twenty minutes before removing and adding a few tablespoons of the beer for moisture. Return to oven for another five minutes; remove and rest to cool.

3. In a large mixing bowl combine the flour, baking powder, and hand-ground spices. Combine the melted butter, egg, sugar, and maple syrup in a separate mixing bowl.

4. Peel the pumpkin, retaining only the flesh; place in a blender. Add half the beer. Pulse in the blender while slowly adding the rest of the beer. You want a milkshake consistency.

5. Pour 1 ⅓ cups of the pumpkin mixture into the wet ingredients bowl and whisk well (reserve the rest for a second batch). Finally dump the dry ingredients into the wet mixture and whisk just until it's a thick batter.

6. Grease your muffin tin and distribute the batter so that each holder is filled nearly to the top. Bake for twelve minutes, remove and rotate the muffins, returning them to bake another ten to twelve minutes, or until starting to brown on the sides.

7. Sweet tooths: garnish with extra maple syrup and orange zest.

BEVERAGE
Alpine Ichabod Ale

SOUNDTRACK
The Fall
"Kurious Oranj"

Delicata Bruschetta

Makes twelve

Our next tattoos just might be "trust farmers." Our friend Aubrey is a certified master gardener (and certified hard-ass) who spent a year working the fields of an upstart organic farm in Massachusetts. So when she walked our LA farmers market with us one winter, we made mental notes of everything she flipped for. Delicata squash, she told us while darting to a distant stand, is her absolute favorite for two reasons. One, its skin is a gorgeous banana-yellow with zebra stripes of candy-corn orange and olive green. Second, this thin skin is delectably edible once roasted. We found a third thing to love about this beauty, something more than skin deep: its soft yellow flesh smells suspiciously like a roasting turkey. Sliced and pumped with a root-vegetable stuffing, these delicata bruschetta are deeply festive, no-kill vessels for stuffing. Leave it to farmers to give us a replacement for frozen tofurkeys. Thanks Aubrey!

2 delicata squashes
2 golden beets
1 small yam
1 green apple
1 white onion
2 stalks celery
½ cup raw pecans
½ cup raw cashews

1 cup and 1 tablespoon
  breadcrumbs
2 cloves garlic
2 tablespoons olive oil
10–12 fresh sage leaves
½ cup vegetable stock
¼ cup Holy Daze Harissa (pg. 49)

1. Start with the stuffing: preheat the oven to 350 degrees. Peel and chop the beets, yam, and onion into small, equal-sized cubes. Chop the celery and green apple slightly smaller. Mix together in a bowl with pecans, cashews, and breadcrumbs. Mince the garlic and make a chiffonade from half the sage leaves; stir with the olive oil before, then add it all to the stuffing bowl. Mix to combine.

2. Spoon the mixture into a well-oiled shallow roasting pan, cover with aluminum foil, and slide into oven to cook. Remove after fifteen minutes and stir, returning to oven for another ten minutes.

3. Once the stuffing has toasted, add the vegetable stock, re-cover, and cook for another fifteen to twenty minutes. Once the yam and beets are cooked through and the stock has cooked off but left the bread gloopy, the stuffing's done. Remove and let cool.

4. Slice the squashes, laying each on your cutting board so that the long ends point horizontally. Now turn the squash slightly upward so you're cutting on a bias, cut into six long slices much like you would a baguette to make long crostini or bruschetta. Each slice should be about an inch thick. Using a spoon, scoop seeds out of each squash slice; be careful not to lose too much flesh.

5. Place squash slices on a well-oiled baking sheet and cook in the oven for about twelve minutes, then remove and flip 'em over and return for another ten minutes. Both sides should have a tinge of brown color but not be fully cooked.

6. Once squash is out of the oven, finish the stuffing mixture by adding harissa and mixing to create a wet and pliable stuffing. Position the squash slices so that the widest side is facing up, and pack with stuffing. Grind the remaining breadcrumbs into a dust and sprinkle on top. Return to the oven until squash and stuffing have gelled and mixture is slightly browning, about fifteen to twenty minutes.

7. Garnish with extra sage leaves and a dash of olive oil.

TIP One of the rad things about involving roots and nuts in your stuffing is that you can kill the bread altogether if need be (for you pesky gluten-free freaks). Simply double the nuts, throw in a second yam for good measure, and if it's not as pliable as you like, up the amount of harissa to act as a binding agent.

BEVERAGE
Telegraph Rhinoceros

SOUNDTRACK
Gram Parsons
"Blue Eyes"

CHEESE

Which cheeses are the best? We've redacted Alex's ninety-eight–page dissertation and truncated our faves down to a few styles worthy of your obsession. Remember, cheap factory-produced cheese tastes like a cheap factory floor. It also snuffs out traditional producers and it champions the abuse of sweet, cuddly dairy animals. Bottom line: find a local cheesemonger or get really into being vegan.

Fresh chèvre is one style of cheese that's great to find locally—just beware the new American cheese producers' goat cheese that doesn't taste "goaty." You're not a baby; don't let them treat you like one. If you buy from overseas, France reigns supreme, but Spain makes some salty licks that rule in their own right.

LOOK FOR: Valençay frais (with ash), Capricho de Cabra, Hillman Farm's chèvre, Vermont Butter and Creamery chèvre.

Alpine cow cheeses are supreme melters and make for standout snacks, plus most of these beasts are produced in conditions that make us get teary with envy and want to run away to Switzerland. Generally, they are cheeses made from cows that live blissed-out summers eating flowers atop mountains.

LOOK FOR: Comté aged a minimum of fourteen months, Beaufort d'alpage, Krümmenswiler bergkäse, Challerhocker, Uplands Pleasant Ridge Reserve.

Rocks, as in hard cheeses, start as 800 pounds of milk and end up an eighty-pound wheel of hard-ass bliss. The rule is simple: never buy Parmigiano-Reggiano that isn't really Parmigiano-Reggiano. The best farms augment their cow's diets with fava beans, corn flakes, and arugula to up protein levels.

LOOK FOR: the needlepoint matrix on the rind. Ask for Bonati and Cravero.

Sheep are the new goat in many ways. Unfortunately for us in the States, not that many ranchers like to deal with these persnickety animals. Those that do know that the fun is in the funk: most sheep's milk cheeses are soft ripened and bloomy as hell, with impressive rinds that taste like the sweaty barnyard they came from.

LOOK FOR: caña de oveja is the gateway drug.

Blues: don't fear 'em. Salty, stinky, weird, some blue cheeses predate Christ. Look for blues that retain their moisture, are sufficiently salty, and have blue veining—yep, that's mold—all the way to the rind. Typically, a blue cheese that crumbles is crap: goo is good.

LOOK FOR: bleu des Causses, Stichelton, queso de Valdeón, Tilston Point, Caveman Blue.

HOT KNIVES

H K

EST. 2005

Rarebit

Serves two (with leftovers)

We refuse to learn that strong hoppy beers make horrible sauces. We should have taken a hint years ago, when we made an onion soup with double-strength Arrogant Bastard ale (double arrogant bastards indeed), and the hop-infused stock tasted so much like licking a rubber tire that we threw out the whole pot and got tacos. And yet, when we set out to make a vegetarian Welsh rarebit (beer and cheese gravy), what did we reach for? Aged Comté and a double India pale ale... an hour later, it too went in the trashcan. A successful rarebit was a long-time coming, but finally we tried the path of moderation and settled on a malty German brew coupled with white cheddar. Don't think this counts as a salad? It is sublime with a thatch of perfect, raw mustard greens nestled on top. There's your greens.

SAUCE

2 tablespoons butter
2 tablespoons all-purpose flour
12 ounces German doppelbock, at room temp
3 teaspoons Wooster Sauce (pg. 63)
6 ounces grated white cheddar (we use Cabot cloth
   bound cheddar)
½ teaspoon white pepper
½ teaspoon cayenne pepper
sea salt to taste

TOAST

2 slices dark rye bread
1 cup fresh baby mustard greens
1 teaspoon olive oil
1 teaspoon grain mustard
2 eggs
fresh cracked black pepper

TIP One of our early drunk experiments lives on! While any egg fanatic will tell you poaching eggs is best done in a water bath mixed with vinegar, we prefer spiking it with beer. But try adding a cup of your doppelbock for a slightly maltier egg.

1. To make the rarebit, set a heavy-bottomed pot on medium heat and add butter. Once bubbly, add flour and stir well until brown. Add beer and stir or whisk well. Let it hit a rolling boil then add the cheese in stages, stirring all the while. Add Wooster first, then white pepper, cayenne, and salt to taste. Remove from heat and set aside or refrigerate for an hour for it to set.

2. Clean and pat your mustard greens dry, picking only the best looking and smaller leaves. If these are massively big, slice them. Pluck off any excess stem. Combine grain mustard and oil in a bowl and whisk. Toss the greens in a bowl with this mustard-emulsion.

3. Slather each slice of bread with rarebit (more than seems wise.) At the same time, bring 4 cups water to a gentle boil, for poaching your eggs.

4. For best poaching, use a slotted spoon to create a whirlpool effect in the water. Then crack your eggs (one at a time) into the center of the whirlpool. Let poach about a minute before removing gently, draining, and setting aside while your toast finishes. (Over easy fried eggs work, too, ya lazy mugs.) Meanwhile, place toast under the broiler for about two minutes; use a pan to catch drippings and watch closely to prevent burning.

5. Plate by setting one slice of toast down first, followed by a handful of mustard greens, slightly off-center, and finally the poached egg directly on the toast, overlapping the salad. Splat on some gravy and grind pepper on top.

BEVERAGE

J.W. Lees Vintage
Harvest Ale

SOUNDTRACK

Buzzcocks
"Why Can't
I Touch It?"

Seven Layer Trip

Serves eight to ten

Come late January, we occasionally hear talk of super bowl this, super bowl that. It has something to do with sports, that much we get (we're not aware of any games). But more importantly, there's talk of a gluttonous food holiday for much of America, and that we can get behind! Now, here's our contribution: seven layers of beans, beer, market produce, molten dairy, spice, herbs, and crunchy protein. It's less a dip and more of a trip—as in LSD—and we're still undecided as to whether it's a good one or bad one. See, we started off calling this monstrosity seven layers of heaven but quickly nicknamed it seven layers of hell (if you make too much and are cursed with leftovers, you will understand). Imagine Dante's infernal rings built out of refried beer beans, chile-cheese Mornay sauce, roasted salsa, avocado-citrus salad, homemade crème fraiche, a bacony dust of pumpkin seeds, and a veritable astroturf of scallion and cilantro. Enjoy the descent!

REFRIED BEANS
½ pound dried pinto beans
3 cups vegetable stock
1 tablespoon grapeseed oil
1 medium yellow onion, chopped
2 garlic cloves, minced
6 chipotle peppers in adobo
½ cup pale ale
salt to taste

1. Make the beans the night before. Bring a large pot filled with the beans and stock to a boil (you need slightly less than double stock to bean ratio) then lower to a simmer and cook for about an hour, or until beans are fork tender. Remove from heat and let sit.

2. In a smaller pot on high heat add the grapeseed oil, then the onion and garlic, stir-ring to keep from burning. Remove the chipotle peppers from their can, roughly chop and add (with sauce) to the pot. Follow with the beer, give a good stir, and add cooked beans without stock (reserve for later). Cook this about ten minutes, just enough for the beer to reduce a bit, and remove from heat. Let cool while you make the cheese sauce.

CHEESE SAUCE
3 Fresno chiles
2 tablespoons butter
2 tablespoons all-purpose flour
2 cups organic milk
8 ounces white cheddar (grated)
1 tablespoons Louisiana hot
   sauce
½ teaspoon turmeric powder
sea salt to taste

1. Burn the chiles directly on your stove top until blackened, then place in a paper bag or Tupperware for five minutes to sweat the skins off. Flake off all black bits and remove seeds, then dice.

2. Put a heavy-bottomed pot on medium heat, add butter and let cook until bubbly, then add flour and stir well. Once it starts to slightly brown, add milk, stir or whisk well, and let continue to cook several minutes. Once you hit a rolling boil, turn to a simmer, and add grated cheddar in stages, stirring all the while. Add hot sauce, turmeric, and salt to taste. Remove from heat and cool.

3. Puree the beer-beans that are now cool using a food processor or handheld mixer. Use some but not all of the leftover stock to blend; if still dry add a tablespoon at a time of stock until creamy. Store both sauces in fridge for at least two hours or overnight.

BEVERAGE

Green Flash Le Freak

SOUNDTRACK

Talking Heads
"Psycho Killer"

SALSA

2 medium hot house tomatoes
1 jalapeño pepper, diced
½ lemon
1 teaspoon olive oil

AVOCADO SALAD

2 ripe Hass avocados
½ lemon
½ mandarin
1 tablespoon olive oil
salt and pepper to taste

OTHER TOPPINGS

½ cup crème fraiche (pg. 62)
¼ cup Magic Shroom Dust
   (pg. 30)
3 green onions
1 cup cilantro leaves

1. Remove your cheese sauce, refried beans, and Magic Shroom Dust from fridge so they warm enough to be easy to work with.

2. Make a simple pico de gallo, dicing tomatoes and jalapeño and mixing with a squeeze of lemon and olive oil. Season as desired. Set aside.

3. Slice avocados lengthwise and then widthwise, leaving one-inch long slices: do so delicately (don't mash, this isn't guac) and add to a mixing bowl with olive oil, the juice and zest of half a mandarin, lemon, and salt and pepper.

4. Finely chop the green onions and cilantro.

5. Assemble by delicately stuffing a small casserole dish or a shaped cutter (a ring mold, or a pie mold work well) with your desired amount of each layer going from beans, to cheese sauce, to salsa, to avocado salad, crème fraiche, mushroom dust, and greens. Serve on a large plate with fresh tortilla chips.

NETTLE MEADOW KUNIK, goat and
cow milk. Thurman, New York

LA PERAL, cow and ewe
milk. Asturias, Spain

Cheeses

AZEITÃO, ewe milk.
Setubal, Portugal

LOU REY FERMIER, ewe milk. Pyrenees, France

CHALLERHOCKER, cow milk. Toggenburg, Switzerland

POINTE DE BIQUE, goat milk. Berry, France

You get what you pay for (Fuck Trader Joe's).

CASATICA DI BUFALA. water buffalo milk. Bergamo, Italy

HOT KNIVES || SALAD DAZE

Belgian Onion Soup

Serves four

In winter, the section of our cupboard devoted to onions seems to grow exponentially, filled with all forms of eye-dripping lovelies: red and white onions, shallots, massive white-bulbed scallions. Grilling a sack of onions down to a cereal bowl of caramelized noodles is a rare fall pleasure. And few pillars of French cooking are as widely and voraciously loved as scalding hot onion soup cloaked in a blistering layer of melted Gruyère. But like with many epic dishes canonized by the cuisine of rural folk, vegetarians usually remain wholly uninvited. So how does one mitigate the beef stock in every single recipe of the gooiest of soups? Our "ah-ha moment" was beer. After trying small batches of all three colors of the proverbial tricolore (blue, white, and red) we settled on Chimay Blue, a dubbel style beer that's become a house-hold name for boozers. This so-called grande réserve, or any other basic dubbel, is a super substitute for the essence of animal gore. The malts and sugars play on your tongue in a way that's strikingly similar to the flavor of liquefied fat and tendon.

        2 tablespoons butter
        2 tablespoons of extra virgin olive oil
        5 large onions, halved and sliced thin
        6 cloves of garlic, minced
        4 shallots, sliced thin
        750 milliliter Chimay Blue
        4 cups vegetable stock
        4 bay leaves
        6 sprigs of thyme
        ½ teaspoon ground white pepper
        4 slices sourdough bread for garnish
        ½ pound Gruyère cheese for garnish
        sea salt to taste

1. Heat a wide pot or cast-iron on medium heat. Add the butter and let it blister.

2. Add the onion and cook uncovered. Let them sit for about four minutes and then stir. Repeat until the onions have all begun to brown, at least twenty minutes.

3. Add the olive oil, garlic, and shallots and stir in the same fashion as before, once every five minutes, until the garlic and shallots have caramelized.

4. Add 2 ½ cups of the beer and crank the heat to just shy of high. Let the beer boil off until there is half as much beer volume as onion volume.

5. Add the stock, bay leaves, thyme leaves, and white pepper. Cook until the liquid has reduced by about two finger widths. Taste the soup and add salt to adjust. Cook for at least an additional twenty minutes before garnishing. In an ideal world, you would let the soup sit a day before serving it. (Just be sure to reheat it.)

6. Take a slice of sourdough and cut it to fit your bowl or cup. Set atop the soup and cover with several slices of Gruyère. Broil until brown and serve hot , topped with extra thyme.

BEVERAGE

De Proef Flemish
Primitive Wild Ale

SOUNDTRACK

Métal Urbain
"Hystérie connective"

Portobello Poutine

Serves six to eight

It felt like a revelation the first time we realized you could wing a killer gravy by using mushrooms instead of meat drippings. Even since that fateful Thanksgiving several years ago, we've been riding the shroom gravy train wherever it takes us, whisking different iterations of oyster and portobello mushroom gravies every year. When an early version of our gravy recipe (one that, quite frankly, lacked precision) disappeared from our blog, we got loads of SOS messages from readers unsure of how to survive the holidays without it—go figure!

But our deeply held belief that mushroom juice is the best umami was elevated to the next level when we separated the process into two separate stages: braising to develop flavors, followed by thickening to create texture. Our technique for braising portobellos is an old reliable formula of booze-vinegar-salt and sweet veggies. But what to do with the remaining, braised mushrooms? We use these juicy tenders to make succulent, breaded portobello fries and the braising liquid to craft a religiously deep and decadent gravy. Once reassembled, this is not far from a poutine of fries and gravy.

BRAISED PORTOBELLOS
4 portobellos
1 tablespoon olive oil
1 carrot
1 stalk celery
½ white onion
1 cup cream sherry
½ cup sherry vinegar
2 tablespoons soy sauce
4 sprigs tarragon

1. Remove the stumpy base from your mushrooms, but leave the gills. Rinse under water and set aside. Chop the carrot, onion and celery. Put a stock pot or cast-iron pot on medium high flame. Add oil and toss in the chopped veg. Stir and cook until barely brown. Add bay leaves.

2. Pour the sherry, soy sauce, and vinegar into the pot. Then add the mushrooms with the gills up. Cover pot with a lid and cook for twenty to thirty minutes on medium heat. Once shrooms are cooked throughout, remove from heat and let sit until cool. To keep: remove mushrooms and place in a bowl or Tupperware, cover them with a couple tablespoons of liquid, and refrigerate (they stay good up to five days).

Continued on next page ⠆

BEVERAGE
Unibrou Maudite

SOUNDTRACK
Leonard Cohen
"Future"

∴ Continued from previous page

DRUNKEN SHROOM GRAVY
¼ pound oyster mushrooms
3 tablespoons butter
  (or margarine)
2 tablespoons all-purpose flour
1 cup braising liquid (above)
1 cup vegetable stock
½ cup heavy cream
1 teaspoon ground sage
1 teaspoon cayenne
sea salt and pepper to taste

1. Place a sauce pot on medium heat and add one tablespoon of butter. Once it's bubbling, tear the oyster mushrooms into the pot, cook and stir for several minutes, until they start to brown and shrivel. Remove and set aside on a plate for later.

2. Return pot to medium heat and add the rest of the butter and scrape any mushroom bits to loosen. Once bubbling, add flour in two separate batches, stirring in between to distribute evenly. Let cook for one minute until flour and butter start to rise and darken in color.

3. Add the reserved braising liquid to the butter-flour roux and stir well. Continue to cook on medium heat until you hit a boil. At that point add stock and heavy cream and keep cooking until it returns to a boil.

4. Place on simmer and cook for ten minutes or until reduced by an inch or so. Add spices and taste. Add salt if needed. Finally return cooked oyster mushrooms and stir. Keep warm until ready to serve.

PORTOBELLO POUTINE
1 cup pastry flour
1 ½ cup panko
1 large egg, beaten
2 cups grapeseed or canola oil
1 cup Drunken Shroom Gravy
4 braised portobellos
1 parsnip, peeled and grated
1 tablespoon fresh horseradish,
  grated (optional)
sea salt to taste

1. Prepare breading supplies by placing pastry flour on a plate, panko bread crumbs, in a shallow bowl, and a beaten egg in a third bowl.

2. Pour frying oil into a deep, heavy-bottomed pot good for frying and place on high heat.

3. Slice each portobello mushroom into six or so long strips and pat dry. Take a handful of these at a time and toss them in pastry flour, coating thoroughly. When all fries are coated, use both hands to take one or two at a time and dip them in egg, lightly flicking off any excess. Finally, gently roll each one in panko crumbs until fully coated. Very lightly tap off any excess crumbs.

4. Fry two fries at a time, dropping them in carefully and letting cook about ten to twenty seconds on each side, or until dark brown and crispy but not burned. Strain out with a spider, drip dry for several seconds, and place on a paper towel near the stove until ready to serve.

5. Make a salad garnish: sprinkle grated parsnip, horseradish and salt on top of fries and serve with gravy for dipping.

Morning Glory Polenta

Serves two

Personally, we find the brunch crush crowding the sidewalks of some LA and New York neighborhoods to be a bum deal. Why would we wait an hour for a table only to be shoved a rushed stack of pancakes, room-temp hashbrowns, and a watered-down mimosa? When we have a powerful urge for a too-large breakfast late in the morning, we stay home. We still love the mimosa—who doesn't? It's like juice and a date drug all in one. All the better to slug at home where you can make food that actually complements such a boozy breakfast. We find something delicate fares better with dry champagne than belly bombs, and wilted arugula over creamy seeded polenta is hearty enough to charm a hungover metalhead and low-cal enough for even *Sex in the City* hags. What's more, it can be dressed up in citrus and champagne.

MORNING GLORY POLENTA
1 cup course-ground cornmeal
¼ cup raw pepitas
¼ sunflower seeds
1 tablespoon sesame seeds
1 small carrot
3 cups vegetable stock
1 teaspoon dried oregano
⅛ teaspoon nutmeg
1 tablespoon margarine
1 teaspoon sea salt
1 teaspoon shredded coconut
5 cups arugula

MIMOSA DRESSING
2 satsuma mandarins
2 tablespoons olive oil
1 teaspoon champagne vinegar
1 teaspoon prosecco (optional)
sea salt to taste

1. Start with the mimosa dressing: grate the zest of one mandarin into a bowl; top the zest off with its juice. Add olive oil and champagne vinegar and whisk together. Finish with a dash of prosecco and salt to taste. Set aside. Peel and supreme the other mandarin.

2. Place your seeds in a cold cast–iron skillet on medium heat, toasting only for five minutes, shaking every thirty seconds to keep from burning. Set aside.

3. Make the polenta: pour stock into a sauce pot and place on high heat. Once you hit a boil, add a third of the polenta and whisk for several minutes. Repeat until all polenta is in the pot, and place on a simmer. Add

nutmeg, oregano, and salt. Texture should be somewhat loose and creamy, though fully cooked. When done, add margarine and stir again. Finally add seeds, grated carrot, and shredded coconut, stir and cover removed from heat.

4. Return the cast–iron skillet to the burner on medium heat and add arugula to wilt. After about thirty seconds, douse in mimosa dressing. Turn off heat and serve.

5. To plate, spoon a half cup of the polenta in a shallow bowl, top with the wilted arugula. Garnish with supremed mandarin slices.

BEVERAGE
Dogfish Head
Festina Pêche

SOUNDTRACK
Brian Eno
"Here Come the
Warm Jets"

Hen & Potatoes

Serves four

We crave chicken thighs like we crave licking salmonella off a spoon, but we'd be liars if we said a rotisserie spit of roasted birds crackling fat over a rack of moist, herbed potatoes didn't look good. We're human, and there's a specific part of the brain wired to respond to fat dripping on potatoes. For this, we found our salvation at a Hollywood–farmers market mushroom stand where they sell head-sized bunches of maitake mushrooms, also known as hen of the woods. Roasted by themselves in an uncovered pan, these beauties shrivel easily, turning from floppy to crispy in a few minutes flat. But dipped in deeply flavored fat and nestled in a cast-iron pan of already sputtering butterballs, these mushrooms literally bloom. Kick in some thyme, sage, and a splash of sherry, and all your hardwired obsessions are satiated.

```
3 bunches maitake mushrooms
2 pounds butterball potatoes
1 tablespoon olive oil
½ white onion
⅛ cup sherry
2 tablespoons "Extra Olive" Olive Oil (pg. 63)
1 teaspoon fresh thyme leaves
1 teaspoon chopped fresh sage
½ cup whole parsley leaves
Green God Oil for garnish (pg. 62)
sea salt to taste
```

1. Preheat oven to 400 degrees and place potatoes whole in the bottom of a Dutch oven or casserole dish with a lid. Coat potatoes evenly with the olive oil and slide into oven with lid on. Cook this way about twelve minutes.

2. Remove the Dutch oven, stir gently and add onion, thyme leaves, chopped sage, and half the well-chopped parsley. Cover and return to the oven for another five to ten minutes or until potatoes are still slightly pert and undercooked.

3. Fill a cereal bowl with "Extra Olive" Olive Oil. Taking each maitake from the base, dip and coat its tops in the oil. Remove the pot from oven and douse potatoes in sherry, then quickly position each maitake bunch standing straight out from the potatoes. Cover with lid and return to the oven about ten minutes. Mushrooms should be wilting and losing shape but still attached.

4. Serve with whole parsley leaves and green god oil, generously salt the fingerlings and crack fresh black pepper on mushrooms.

TIP The beauty of this dish is lost if you slaughter the hen: keep her in one piece. That starts by bringing a separate small handbag to the market when you're buying hen of the woods mushrooms. If they're sold in a brown sack, carry that by hand. To cook, dress the mushrooms carefully and gingerly prop them up in your dutch oven using the potatoes. Serve the whole roasted bouquets with a steak knife so you can slice off in sections over the potatoes.

BEVERAGE

The Bruery Rugbrød

SOUNDTRACK

Fear
"Meat and Potatoes"

BEER

When pairing, chugging, and cooking we've always preferred grains to grapes. Back when we were young, we had to walk a mile off-campus through the pounding heat just to find a liquor store that carried Rogue ales. But now that good beer's having a heyday, and we can find our favorite Belgian beers at 7-Eleven, being an informed consumer is all the more vital so you're not swindled by poseurs.

Shopping for beer should feel more like buying a gun and less like stocking up on instant ramen at Costco; it's an investment and an experience, not a chore. Find stores that show respect by offering a curated selection beyond what big distributors push on them. Telltale signs: bottles you've seen nowhere else, high-turnover on shelves, seasonal ales exploding around fall.

To really know beer, say "yes" to risk and "no" to monogamy. Don't head for the beer you already love. We swore off six-packs long ago in an effort to taste everything. Think of it as swinging.

Pairing food with beer is a subjective game. Pick organizing principles and use them as guides but always test those limits. We love IPAs with Alpine cheeses, sheep's milk with sour ales, and blues with barleywines—except when we don't! Are you going for how the beer alters the cheese, echoes it, destroys it? Sometimes beers have a vibe, an attitude, a certain unspoken sumthin' that can't be captured in a "flavor profile." For those times, you must pair from a carnal place.

Winter warmers can verge on overplayed. While high-octane barley-wines feel good in cold months, subtler beers can rule your short days too. We like substituting a gueuze for wine at the Thanksgiving dinner table, a saison for morning mimosas, and extra-hopped West Coast IPA while trudging through the snow.

When you cook with beer, you play with fire. There are flavors here that you don't encounter with wine, mistakes will be made (and soups and sauces will be dumped). Try replacing the dairy in baking, the wine in braising, and the stock in pressure-cooking. Avoid cooking with any beer with "extra" or "double" in the name.

Aging beer is the final frontier. Whether you get a converted wine cooler, rent a storage locker, or—like us—find a dank old chest and lug it into your bedroom closet, follow these simple rules: 1) nothing "freshly hopped" 2) always upright 3) dark as night 4) constant temp 5) drink one, save one.

Banana Beer Bread

Makes one loaf

We accidentally fed this bread to the only American food critic who's won a Pulitzer Prize—Jonathon Gold—and he seemed to like it okay. What happened was that we had brewed an illegal beer with tonka beans, this South American seed pod that contains a chemical that is lethal in large doses but tastes delicious in small ones (like marzipan and cinnamon), so we were invited to pour our illicit homebrew at a speakeasy in Downtown LA where Gold was hosting a VIP beer tasting. But we ran into him out on the street while lugging in our keg and a couple trays of beer desserts. Our friend, who shall remain nameless, is a big fan of Gold, and grasping for anything he could think of to strike up a conversation, nearly shoved the banana bread he was holding down the esteemed food critic's gullet. "Oh god, it's made with margarine," we thought as we watched this pork-belly obsessed gourmand finger it. "You can really taste the beer," is all he said. Vegans, take note.

2 cups all-purpose flour
2 teaspoons baking powder
1 teaspoon salt
3 over-ripe bananas
½ cup margarine, melted
½ cup barley malt syrup (or white sugar)
1 ½ cup hefeweizen, room temp
1 tablespoon whole cloves
1 teaspoon whole coriander
1 teaspoon ground cinnamon
½ teaspoon ground nutmeg
zest of one orange
zest of one lemon
1 tablespoon Belgian candi sugar
   (or more barley malt syrup)

1. Measure out your flour and baking powder and stir in a large mixing bowl. Preheat oven to 350 degrees.

2. In a second large mixing bowl, combine wet ingredients and spices: peel and mash your ripe 'naners and combine with melted margarine. Add malt syrup or sugar and the beer while stirring with a spatula.

3. Grind coriander and clove in a mortar and pestle or coffee grinder (or simply with a knife) and add to the wet ingredients along with cinnamon and nutmeg. Finally, zest an

orange and a lemon over your cutting board. Add half of each to the bowl, and reserve half for garnish.

4. Combine wet and dry ingredients and mix well, stirring until lumps disappear. Pour batter into a canola or margarine-greased bread pan. Bake at 350 degrees for forty to fifty minutes. Test the middle; it should be moist but not wet. Remove and immediately cool on a cooling rack to prevent burnt bottom. Rub the Belgian candi sugar or barley malt syrup on top, and sprinkle with zest for garnish. Serve warm.

BEVERAGE
Franziskaner
Hefe-Weisse

SOUNDTRACK
Bonnie Raitt
"Mighty Tight Woman"

HOT KNIVES | SALAD DAZE

Beer Candied Apples

Serves six

It's inordinately hard to gross us out, but we almost gagged when our friend Molly first told us about the way her Manhattanite, Jewish uncle would cook red apples in Cherry Coke: he'd core the apples and wrap them in tinfoil, using the soda as a braising liquid. Our revulsion quickly turned to attraction when we realized this could just as easily be done with beer. Since then, we've tried braising pommes with everything from apple beer to hard cider and dark beers, but we have learned to use a light hand: we prefer a slightly spiced farmhouse-style saison. Something with citrus peel notes is good; anything with coriander is best. The real surprise here is how stuffing a coriander crumble inside and on top of the apples cements them in a beer-sugar syrup and injects a pie crust inside each orb, giving it a gooey center.

> 6 medium Fuji apples
> 1 cup beer (saison)
> ¾ cup all-purpose flour
> 1 stick butter (room temp)
> ½ cup brown sugar
> zest of one lemon
> 2 tablespoons fresh coriander seeds
> sea salt to taste

1. Preheat the oven to 350 degrees and prepare the apples by coring them.

2. Place the apples next to one another in a medium-sized casserole dish. Measure out the beer and pour it into the middle of each apple; it's fine if it escapes slowly, but some should pool inside. Cover the apples with aluminum foil and stick them in the oven. Cook this way for about ten minutes.

3. While you wait, make the crumble: in a small skillet, heat the fresh coriander seeds on medium heat, shaking every thirty seconds to keep from scorching. Once aromatic, remove from heat and let sit for a minute. Transfer to a mortar and pestle (or clean coffee grinder) and turn into powder. Add to a large mixing bowl with flour, warm butter, lemon zest, and brown sugar. Mix well with your fingers.

4. Check on apples; the beer should be starting to boil up. Remove the foil and cook for another five minutes. Finally, remove and carefully fill each apple's hollow core with the crumble, pressing down to fit as much in as possible. Sprinkle any remaining crumble around the apples in the beer. Stick back in the oven for another fifteen minutes. Remove as soon as crumble appears to brown on top and before apples fall apart.

TIP If you're hard core you prolly don't have an apple corer, here's what you want to do: take a paring knife, make a half-inch incision near the stem and curve the knife around 360 degrees to pop it out. Once you do, plunge the knife deeper and gently wiggle it in a neat, circular fashion to churn out the core and seeds, until you've created a tunnel to the other side. Using a chef's knife, slice the very base of each apple off so that they sit flat.

BEVERAGE
Dupont Avec Les
Bons Vœux

SOUNDTRACK
Silver Apples
"Ruby"

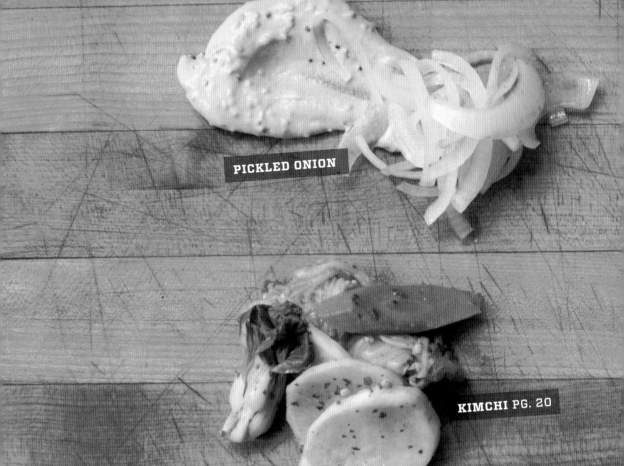

PICKLED ONION

KIMCHI PG. 20

"Charcuterie"

Put the crude in "crudités."

SEITAN SLICES PG. 71

FENNEL KRAUT PG. 74

BLOOD SAUSAGE
MUSHROOMS PG. 110

FAUX GRAS PG. 54

109

Blood Sausage Mushrooms

Makes six

There's little pleasure in textured soy; no mystique to black bean patties. This, above all else, is why we've steered clear of fake meats ever since our early years of giving up real flesh. We find more inspiration in the dark-matter nether regions of nature (i.e. funghi, root bulbs, fatty seeds). But we never said we were scared of blood... When the two of us were prep cooks at our college mess hall, one of our favorite pranks involved cow's blood. We'd finish slicing beef for the grill station and be left with a metal tray of stinking red mess, so we'd take turns dipping our hands into the blood bath and leaving handprints all over our pressed white jackets. Then we'd pick up a box of romaine and some baby corn, head out of the kitchen and nonchalantly walk to the dining room to refill the salad bar while suntanned babes in J Crew pajamas looked on in horror. We are not above these shenanigans now, either. Which is what led to our most awesome discovery: you can make mushrooms bleed by soaking them in a simple solution of salted beet juice and searing in the color. On your plate these sausage-sized mushrooms only reveal their secret when sliced and pressed with silverware, their blood gathering on your knife. Is it really worth making a twelve-hour marinade to reconnect with food that bleeds? We think so. Is it worth it to gross out your righteous vegan friends? Yes, yes it is.

TIP To score the mushrooms, gently slice about an eighth inch deep with long knife strokes, then rotate the mushroom 180 degrees so that when you repeat this motion it creates a crosshatch design. Pretend you're handling a meat that needs to be penetrated with marinade.

Beverage

Stone Sublimely Self-Righteous Ale

SOUNDTRACK

Soft Cell
"Sex Dwarf"

BLOOD BATH
6 king oyster mushrooms
4 red beets
¼ cup water
2 teaspoons kosher salt

THE BRAISE
3 tablespoons grapeseed oil
1 tablespoon fennel seeds, crushed
1 tablespoon smoked paprika
½ white onion
½ cup Madeira wine
¼ cup red wine vinegar
1 tablespoon soy sauce

1. Make the blood bath marinade: trim and peel your beets and place them in a food processor. Pulse for thirty seconds to thoroughly destroy them. Stop and start again, this time pouring in water as you go to help the mixture move. Pulse this way for one minute, wiping down the sides if necessary to make sure all the beet bits dissolve. Once liquefied, remove, strain through a fine mesh strainer discarding pulp and keeping liquid. Salt to taste, using about 2 teaspoons of salt.

2. Next, prepare the mushrooms. Take each king oyster mushroom and slice off the cap and base just enough to get rid of woody parts (reserve the cap for later use). Now score the king oysters.

3. Lay the king oysters in a large container with a lid, cover with beet blood. Cover and store for twelve hours, flipping over after the first three hours.

· · · · · · · · *12 Hours Later* · · · · · · · ·

4. Prepare the mushrooms for braising by shaking excess blood off and sitting for several minutes in 2 tablespoons grapeseed oil, the fennel, and the paprika. Heat a heavy-bottomed pot with remaining oil and sauté the chopped onion for several minutes. Add the mushrooms and stir for a minute before adding vinegar and soy sauce. Cover and cook for twelve to fifteen minutes, stirring often. Remove from heat and keep covered ten more minutes. At this point you can use the mushrooms immediately or store them for three to four days.

5. To finish, heat a new skillet with additional grapeseed oil. Pat mushrooms dry and place in pan. Sear for a couple minutes on each side. Remove from heat and let sit on a wooden cutting board before cutting open and serving.

Psychedelic Rice

Serves four

If you close your eyes and imagine the most trippy food you can think of—kombucha mother, raw oysters, corn fungus—you're probably not thinking of rice. Once you cook this tie-dye, stir-fry, jungle-tropics rice explosion, though, it will top anything else you can conjure up. Staring into a bowl of these three dark grains mixed is like being on your back transfixed by the cottage cheese ceiling of your parents' basement while it crawls with acid trails. Waiting for them to cook takes about as long as your magic mushrooms to sneak up. But let's be honest, the real treat is the salad's ecstatic color wheel: staring into the kiwi emerald green globs, swirling gold and magenta beets, and vaginal pink kale—all sticking out of a deep-purple quinoa abyss that also emits neon-green fractals of Romanesco broccoli—is an exercise in holding onto your sanity, like peaking at a Phish concert. Though not unpleasurable, this one is for those of you who can keep your shit together in public when hard drugs take hold.

KIWI GREMOLATA
1 large kiwi
2 tablespoons grapeseed oil
2 tablespoons olive oil
¼ teaspoon habanero pepper, minced
1 tablespoon chopped flat-leaf parsley
½ teaspoon sea salt

RICE
1 cup forbidden rice
1 cup wild rice
½ cup red quinoa

4 cups filtered water
1 tablespoon butter or margarine
¼ cup raw peanuts
¼ cup raw pistachios
1 teaspoon grapeseed oil

SALAD
1 cup purple flowering kale
1 golden beet
1 red beet
2 tablespoons red wine vinegar
1 head Romanesco broccoli
¼ cup golden raisins

1. Roast the beets by wrapping in foil and cooking at 375 degrees until fork tender, thirty to forty minutes. Once roasted, unwrap, peel, and slice the beets with a mandolin; set the two colored beets together in the fridge to cool—overlap the colors!

2. To make the gremolata, peel your kiwi and then gently dice into small cubes. Combine in a small bowl with chopped parsley, oils, and minced chile. Salt to taste and set in fridge until you serve.

3. Cook the forbidden rice and wild rice together, adding one cup of each to 3 ½ cups of water. Place on medium-high heat and add margarine or butter. Once pot hits a boil, lower to a simmer and cover. Cook as directed depending on the rice—about forty-five minutes—and set aside. In a separate, smaller pot cook the red quinoa by combining half a cup with one cup of water and bring to a boil; cover and simmer for eight to ten minutes, set aside.

4. Wash and dry flowering kale and slice into long slivers. Place in a bowl with red wine vinegar to marinate until you're ready to use.

5. Combine raw pistachios and peanuts in a skillet on high heat; roast for about ten minutes, tossing every few minutes to keep from burning. Remove from heat and sit several minutes to fully cook and cool.

6. Cook the Romanesco: bring a pot of salted water to a bowl and dunk for about a minute to lightly blanche.

7. Place a skillet on high heat with grapeseed oil. Add rices, quinoa, and nuts and stir-fry for about five minutes, stirring often; don't let the rice to stick. Remove and combine in a mixing bowl with the raisins, chilled beet slices and marinated kale.

8. Plate by topping with Romanesco and drizzling with kiwi gremolata.

BEVERAGE

Williams Brothers
Fraoch 20th
Anniversary Ale

SOUNDTRACK

Acid Mothers Temple
"Dark Stars in the
Dazzling Sky"

New Year Peas

Serves ten to twelve

What New Year's Eve is complete without a California blackeye? Yes, we usually drink enough on December 31 to burst sensitive blood vessels, but we're talking about the California black-eye, a bean varietal that you probably know by its confiscated common name, the black-eyed pea. Often cooked up for good luck with ham and pepper sauce, black-eyed peas help end the year with a zing. Since we can't see what makes a hog's jowl floating in your cowpeas lucky, we focus on crafting the most concentrated pepper broth this side of the Mason-Dixon line: deep-emerald poblano peppers and a few hotter chiles lend it color and heat, while tomatillos provide the acid and a thick, globular richness. Slurp too many suds alongside these though, and the next morning you're decidedly not going to feel lucky.

> 1 pound black-eyed peas, dry
> 4 poblano peppers
> 4 tomatillos
> 2 yellow wax peppers
> 2 jalapeños
> 1 tablespoon grapeseed oil
> 8 cups veggie stock (pg. 30)
> 1 red bell peppers
> 2 tablespoons mayonnaise, if desired (pg. 62)
> sea salt to taste

1. Dump black-eyed peas in a bowl, pick out duds and cover with warm water for thirty minutes.

2. Prepare chiles for roasting by preheating oven to 350 degrees and slicing open the poblano, wax, and jalapeño peppers. Using your knife, or your fingers if you have a latex glove, pry out the seeds and discard, along with stems. Place the halved peppers on an oiled piece of tin foil, and place it on a baking sheet along with the tomatillos, skins and all. Roast for thirty minutes or until peppers start to brown and tomatillos deflate slightly. Set aside to cool for a few minutes.

3. Once cooled, put peppers and tomatillos in a blender or food processor. Add one cup of vegetable stock to help it move and begin pulsing. Slowly add three more cups of stock and blend for at least one minute to ensure velvety texture. Salt to taste and pulse again.

4. Strain by pouring through a mesh strainer, in two or three batches, into a bowl. As you pour, rub the puree through by pressing down in a circular motion with a ladle. Clear the strainer of pulp and repeat. Set aside.

5. Combine the black-eyed peas in a pot with the remaining four cups of stock (if it isn't double the volume of your peas, add water) and cook on high heat. Once you hit a boil, turn to low and cook for about forty to fifty minutes or until peas are tender. Immediately strain and discard stock liquid. Rinse the pot and return peas to it; add the pepper broth and return to medium heat.

6. Prepare a fire-roasted red bell pepper garnish by placing pepper directly on a burner. Char each side and turn every couple minutes. Once black on all sides, place in a paper bag or plastic container with a lid, and let cool. After several minutes. Remove skin by rubbing with your hands. Slice into match-stick–thin slices. Set aside.

7. Once peas and pepper broth reaches a boil, turn off, stir and serve. Garnish with a dollop of mayonnaise and strips of bell pepper.

BEVERAGE

Mikkeller Tomahawk

SOUNDTRACK

Big Country
"In a Big Country"

Coco Panna Cotta

Serves four to six

Dessert has long been our final frontier; we typically relegate the dessert plate to cheese, fruit, or booze, or some blissful ménage of the three. We rarely create what could be typified as pastry-chef concoctions. But a run-in with the shimmering glory of a proper panna cotta, that Italian cream-dream thickened with gelatin, made our heads swim with visions of how to perfect our own version for the vegan sweet tooth. Serendipity, and inspiration, struck one day while we were wandering the aisles of our local Vietnamese grocer, a strange smelling depot called A-Market. Staring at us were cans of coconut milk and plastic wrapped agar agar, a vegan, seaweed-based gelatin stand-in. The resulting creamy gel is a simple but totally seductive lipid-and-sucrose jiggler that supports all manner of fruits and sauces. To satisfy our booze and fruit cravings, we like to match this with slices of bourbon-infused pear and top with bourbon peppercorns. Play at will.

1 ½ cups coconut milk
2 fresh vanilla beans
½ cup honey or agave nectar
4 grams agar agar
1 cup water

1 ⅛ cups bourbon
1 Bartlett pear, quartered
1 blood orange
1 tablespoon bourbon
    peppercorns (pg. 44)

1. Start your pear the day before: take a jar with a lid and stuff the quartered pear inside, and fill with bourbon until it covers the pear. Set on the counter overnight.

· · · · · · · · *24 Hours Later* · · · · · · · ·

2. To make panna cotta, empty the cans of coconut milk into a medium sauce pot and heat on low. Split vanilla bean pods and scrape the contents into the milk, then toss in the pods too. Add honey and continue to heat for ten to fifteen minutes, until the milk begins to bubble—do not boil. When it's hot and sudsy, remove from heat and set aside to cool. When the milk is cool (about thirty minutes) it will be well infused with the vanilla.

3. In a smaller sauce pot, heat the cup of water on high heat until it boils. Reduce the heat to just below boiling and add the agar agar while stirring rapidly. Agar agar melts at a very high temperature, but if you boil it you'll lose water, which will upset the ratio. If you have powdered agar, add it all at once and stir until it seems to have dissolved. If you have sticks, break them off into little chunks (you can jam them in a food processor to make it quick) and do the same.

4. Fish the vanilla pods out of your coconut milk, then combine the hot agar gel with the coconut milk and whisk thoroughly. Dump equal servings (about a quarter cup) into your serving vessels, and place in the fridge to cool. Depending on your fridge temp, this should not take longer than thirty to sixty minutes.

5. Garnish with sliced bourbon pear, blood orange segments, and any other fresh fruit, plus cracked bourbon peppercorns.

TIP Agar agar is available in stick and powder form; usually you'll find sticks at Asian markets. While the sticks require a little more labor, they are cheaper than the powder. Make sure that you have serving vessels picked out before you start making the panna cotta. We like small serving cups, but if you prefer to turn the finished gel upside down onto a plate, which is traditional, try a bowl. Leftovers can be frozen or pureed into smoothies or shakes.

BEVERAGE

Uncommon
Siamese Twin

SOUNDTRACK

Sonic Youth
"My Friend Goo"

Hot Squash Ice Cream

Serves four

The mad scientist bros behind the most notorious molecular gastronomy kitchen in the world—elBulli in Spain—can transform vegetables into air, fruits into gasses, and meats into cotton candy. But they've admitted publicly there's one substance that has 'em stumped: hot ice cream. Apparently sodium nitrate and bicalcium phosphate don't work. We think they may be trying too hard. It's the kind of problem that can be solved by splitting a butternut squash in half, roasting it until it's soft, and scooping out its orange flesh into big Ben and Jerry's–sized scoops. Doused with mulled maple syrup and the crunchy sugared and spiced pecan dust, this feels like unearthing a desert straight out of the snow-packed earth. To use every last drop of sustenance, we turn the remaining pecan milk into a warm horchata shooter.

PECAN DIRT AND HORCHATA SHOT
1 cup raw pecans
2 cups filtered water
4 tablespoons brown sugar
1 teaspoon ground cardamom
1 teaspoon ground cinnamon
½ teaspoon fresh nutmeg

HOT SQUASH "ICE CREAM"
1 butternut squash
¼ cup stout beer
mulled maple syrup (pg. 63)
sea salt to taste
canola spray

1. Prepare pecan dirt and horchata by soaking the pecans in filtered water overnight on the counter in a container with a lid.

2. The next day, strain the pecans over a bowl to separate nuts from the pecan milk. Then place nuts in a food processor, pulse, and slowly drizzle pecan milk back in to help them move. Pulse for several minutes. Stop and let sit for several minutes.

3. Re-strain the mixture by pouring into a fine mesh strainer placed over a bowl; press all the moisture out of the pecan pulp.

4. Preheat the oven to 200 degrees. Spread the pecan pulp onto parchment paper on a baking sheet and slide into the oven to cook for thirty minutes, removing to stir with a spoon every five minutes.

5. Pour the strained nut milk into a sauce pot and place over medium heat. To the milk, add 2 tablespoons brown sugar, and the cinnamon, and nutmeg. Once the milk boils, whisk and set to a simmer for several minutes. Keep warm until ready to serve.

6. After thirty minutes of stirring pecan dirt, remove and add 2 tablespoons brown sugar and cardamom. Salt to taste. Pulse this mixture yet again; keep warm until ready to serve.

7. Preheat oven to 350 degrees. Split the squash and remove seeds carefully with a spoon.

8. Place squash face down in a roasting dish sprayed with canola oil, cover with foil. Cook for about 15 minutes and remove to test by pressing against the backside. It should react slightly to your touch, like a ripe avocado. Remove foil and splash with beer. Return to oven for five to eight minutes or until slightly more supple. Remove and flip over, flesh should be bright orange but not caramelized.

9. Plate by scattering a bit of pecan dirt carefully around the plate. Using an ice cream scoop, dig out several tablespoons for each serving and place scoops. Top with another handful of pecan dirt, maple syrup, and a dash of sea salt and serve with warm horchata.

BEVERAGE
La Trappe Quadrupel Koningshoeven

SOUNDTRACK
The Amps
"Pacer"

⬤ HK Playlist

Acid Mothers Temple: "Dark Stars in the Dazzling Sky," from *Have You Seen the Other Side of the Sky?* (Ace Fu, 2006), **113**

Air: "J'ai dormi sous l'eau," from *Premiers symptomes* (Virgin, 1999), **65**

Althea & Donna: "Uptown Top Ranking," from *Uptown Top Ranking* (Frontline, 1978), **30**

The Amps: "Pacer," from *Pacer* (4AD/Elektra, 1995), **118**

Devendra Banhart: "Fall," from *Rejoicing in the Hands* (Young God, 2004), **85**

Belle & Sebastian: "The Model," from *Fold Your Hands Child, You Walk Like a Peasant* (Matador, 2000), **50**

Big Country: "In a Big Country," from *The Crossing* (Mercury, 1983), **114**

Built To Spill: "Distopian Dream Girl," from *There's Nothing Wrong With Love* (Up, 1994), **81**

Buzzcocks: "Why Can't I Touch It?" from *A Different Kind of Tension* (Mute, 1979), **91**

The Clash: "Safe European Home," from *Give 'Em Enough Rope* (Sony, 1979), **73**

Leonard Cohen: "Future," from *The Future* (Columbia, 1992), **99**

The Cure: "If Only Tonight We Could Sleep," from *Kiss Me, Kiss Me, Kiss Me* (Fiction, 1987), **82**

The Deeep: "Mudd," from *Muddy Tracks* (100% Silk, 2011), **45**

Dinosaur Jr.: "Freak Scene," from *Bug* (SST, 1988), **41**

EC8OR: "Gimme NyQuil All Night Long," from *Dynamite* (Edel Records, 2000), **35**

Electric Hellfire Club: "Incubus (Lætherstrip Remix)," from *Calling Dr. Luv* (Cleopatra, 2004), **71**

Brian Eno: "Here Come the Warm Jets," from *Here Come the Warm Jets* (EMI, 1974), **101**

The Fall: "Kurious Oranj," from *I Am Kurious Oranj* (Beggars Banquet, 1988), **87**

Serge Gainsbourg: "Aux armes et cætera," from *Aux armes et cætera* (Polygram, 1979, **68**

Girls' Generation: "Gee," from *Gee* (SM Entertainment, 2010), **22**

Tsegué-Maryam Guèbrou: "Mother's Love," from *Ethiopiques, Vol. 21* (Buda Musique, 2006), **76**

Françoise Hardy: "Tous les garçons et les filles," from *The Yeh-Yeh Girl from Paris!* (BMG International, 1965), **58**

Hot Chip: "Ready for the Floor," from *Made in the Dark* (EMI, 2008), **27**

Inca Ore with Lemon Bear's Orchestra: "The Birds in the Bushes," from *The Birds in the Bushes* (5 Rue Christine, 2006), **57**

The Jesus and Mary Chain: "Happy When It Rains," from *Darklands* (Warner Bros., 1987), **67**

Fear: "Meat and Potatoes," from *Have Another Beer with Fear* (Hall of Records, 1995), **103**

Fela Kuti: "Gentleman," from *Music Is the Weapon of the Future, Vol. 2* (Ex Works, 1998), **84**

The Make-Up: "I Am If..." from *I Want Some* (K Records, 1999), **25**

Neu!: "Neuschnee," from *Neu! 2* (Gronland, 1973), **74**

Nirvana: "Sliver," from *Sliver* (Tupelo Records, 1990), **75**

Métal Urbain: "Hystérie connective," from *Les hommes mort sont dangereux* (Byzanteen, 1981), **97**

The Muslims: "Walking With Jesus," from *Parasites/ Walking With Jesus* (I Hate Rock 'N' Roll, 2008), **86**

Os Mutantes: "Baby," from *Os Mutantes* (Omplatten, 1968), **19**

Gram Parsons with The International Submarine Band: "Blue Eyes," from *Safe at Home* (LHI, 1968), **89**

Pictureplane: "Cyclical Cyclical (Atlantis)," from *Dark Rift* (Lovepump United, 2009), **54**

Primal Scream: "If They Move, Kill 'Em," from *Vanishing Point* (Sire/Creation, 1997), **53**

Bonnie Raitt: "Mighty Tight Woman," from *Bonnie Raitt* (Rhino, 1971), **105**

The Rolling Stones: "Sweet Black Angel," from *Exile on Main St.* (Virgin, 1972), **44**

♟ HK Beer List

AleSmith Decadence 75

Allagash Fluxus 84

Alpine Ichabod Ale 87

Avery Kaiser Imperial Oktoberfest Lager 29

Avery Maharaja Imperial IPA 45

Bear Valley Black Flag Imperial Stout 57

Bell's Kalamazoo Stout 77

The Bruery Mischief 37

The Bruery Rugbrød 103

Craftsman Aurora Borealis 35

Craftsman Cabernale 86

De Proef Flemish Primitive Wild Ale 97

Dogfish Head Festina Pêche 101

Dupont Avec Les Bons Vœux 107

Fantôme Spéciale de Nöel 49

Franziskaner Hefe-Weisse 105

Gouden Carolus Cuvée Van de Keizer Blauw 71

Green Flash Le Freak 92

Hair of the Dog Fred From the Wood 55

Hitachino Nest XH 43

Jolly Pumpkin Oro de Calabaza 19

J.W. Lees Vintage Harvest Ale 91

Kulmbacker Eisbock 50

Lagunitas Brown Shugga' 76

Lagunitas Hop Stoopid Ale 27

La Trappe Quadrupel Koningshoeven 118

Lindemans Cherry Kriek 53

Lindemans Gueuze Cuvée René 74

Lost Abbey Angel's Share 44

Maui CoCoNut Porter 73

McEwan's Scotch Ale 31

Mikkeller Beer Geek Brunch 41

Mikkeller Tomahawk 114

New Belgium La Folie 51

Oskar Blues GUBNA Imperial IPA 20

Port Midnight Sessions Lager 30

Port Santa's Little Helper 85

Pretty Things Saint Botolph's Town Rustic Dark Ale 38

Rodenbach Classic Red 68

Russian River Blind Pig IPA 22

Russian River Temptation 54

Schmaltz He'Brew Bittersweet Lenny's R.I.P.A. 81

Stone Sublimely Self-Righteous Ale 110

Stone, Victory, and Dogfish Head Saison du BUFF 67

Telegraph Rhinoceros 89

Telegraph Stock Porter 65

Uehara Shuzou Echigo Stout 25

Uncommon Siamese Twin 117

Unibrou Maudite 99

Verhaeghe Duchesse de Bourgogne 58

Westvleteren 12 82

Williams Brothers Fraoch 20th Anniversary Ale 113

Index

Acknowledgments

Evan offers his loudest love to Meagan Yellott—for devouring what I cook, inspiring it to better, and always being there to help clean up life's messes. Also, thank you parents for giving me a stellar education even while I seemed destined to toss salads for a living.

Alex thanks the love of his life, Lake Elinore Sharp, for every iota of her being: You've made me one hell of a man. Mom and Dad: thanks for life and your unflinching support. Thanks to the drug-addled, tattooed cooks from my teens who taught me to work, and Marcia Homiak for showing me its meaning.

HOT KNIVES EXTENDS OUR DEEPEST DANKEST THANKS TO THE FOLLOWING RULERS OF OUR UNIVERSE:

Amanda Marsalis and Jen Wick

Mikey, Jonah, Steve, Claire, Curt, and everyone at UrbanHonking

Father Votor & the Elf Family

Steve and Nicole Grandjean

Mark Batty: Buzz, Jake, and Christopher

Ryan Sweeney and the Verdugo Bar, the Beer Chicks, Alex Macy

Molly Rodgeveller, Dave Stickel, and the dudes at quarrygirl.com

Aubrey White, Greg Buss, Tim Walker, Michael, and Lesley Bargar Suter, Mike Dunn, Matthew Spencer and Laura Wing, J. Todd Walker, Kimberly Reiss.

Martin and Ariel Albornoz

Chef Joe Parks and Doug Westin

Kate and Sage

Ha's Apple Farm, Beylik Farms, Jazzy Sprouts, Arreola Farm, and of course Yang Farms for their amazing Napa cabbages.

Alex Brown & Evan George

Alex Brown currently holds court as the general manager for Gourmet Imports, where he answers the questions, and tempers the fury, of the best chefs, cheesemongers, and restaurateurs in Los Angeles. He's an expert frequently quoted on cheese by food publications including *Imbibe*, the *LA Weekly*, and the *Los Angeles Times*. A long-standing line cook vet, Brown took his first cooking job at age 14 as dishwasher/prep cook/garde-manger at the now extinct Indigo Crow Bistro in Albuquerque, New Mexico. His innate obsession with ales began as a baby: his mother routinely drank Guinness Export prior to breastfeeding (thanks, Ma). When he's not importing obscure cheeses, sniffing truffles, vetting olive oils, or being a brute, he headbangs in the internationally renowned sludge band Robedoor, and is an avid lover of cycling.

Evan George is an investigative journalist whose coverage of the health insurance industry, homelessness, and the federal court system has won local and national awards—none of which have stemmed from his extensive writing about beer, coffee, and cooking for publications including *Los Angeles* magazine, *Condé Nast Traveler*, and the *Los Angeles Times*. Born and raised outside of Washington DC, George credits his formative high school years drinking beer in Berlin, Germany, for his love for strong suds. He has grilled steaks at a Philadelphia bistro, flipped burgers in LA coffee shops, and, most recently, spent three years as a sous chef at the renowned vegetarian hot spot Elf Cafe. He holds a history degree from Occidental College.

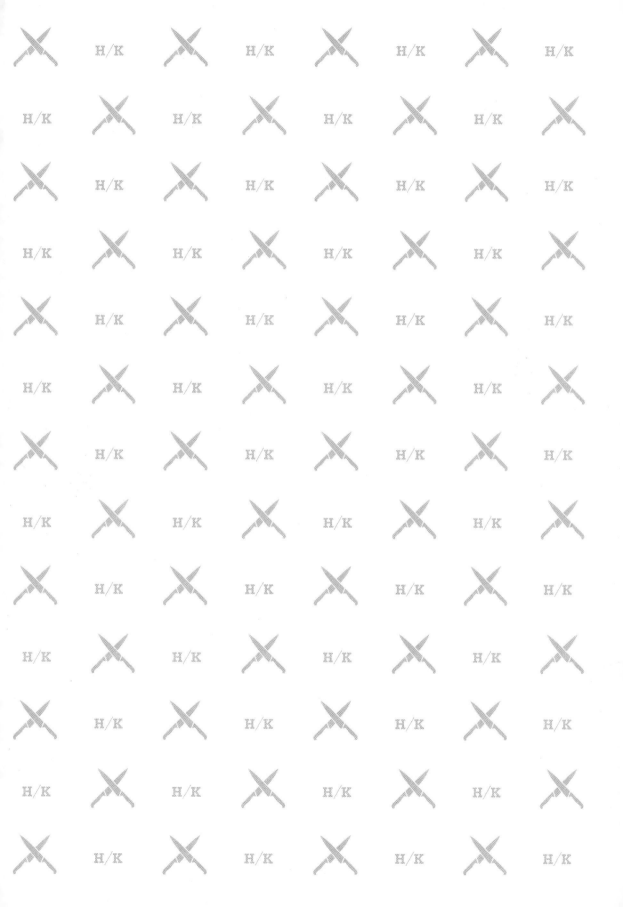

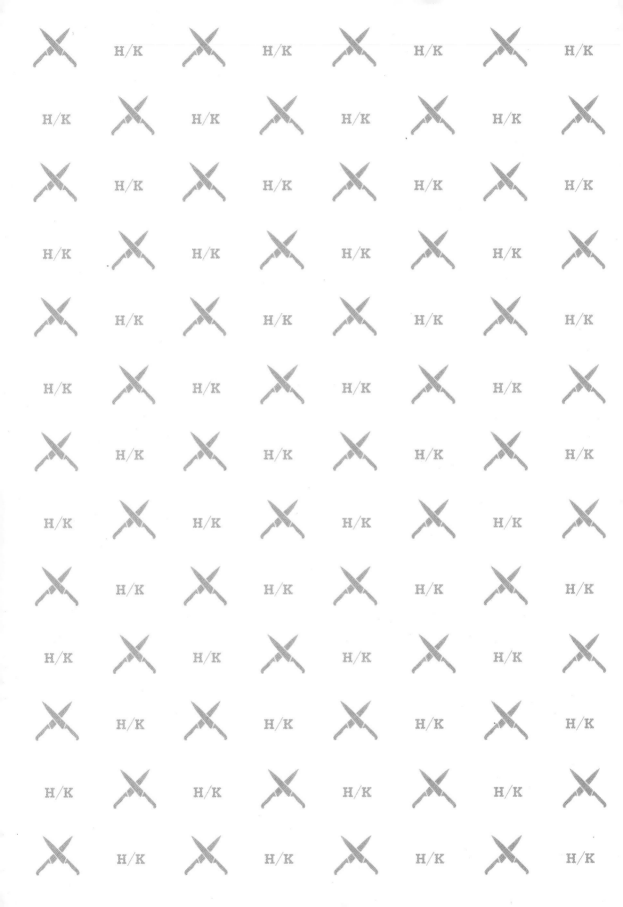